ABBA®

GOLD

The Complete Story

by

JOHN TOBLER

St. Martin's Press
New York

First published in Great Britain by
Century 22 Ltd, Pinewood Studios, Iver Heath, Bucks, SL0 0NH

Published under license from Polar Music International AB, Sweden.
Photographs copyright Polar Music International AB, Sweden.

ISBN 0-312-11227-0

First Edition
10 9 8 7 6 5 4 3 2 1

Written by: John Tobler
Created by: Keith Shackleton
Edited by: Dick Wallis
Art and design direction by: Kevin Cann
Photo research by: Marianne Wallis

The publishers and author gratefully acknowledge the help and cooperation of the following, who all contributed in various ways.
They are listed alphabetically:
Marc Abbott, Ruth Blacktop, Cheryl Bourke, Carole Broughton, Kevin Cann, Florrie Knowles, Alex Duval-Smith, Lucy Etherington, Chris Griffin,
Görel Hanser, George McManus, Lynda Morrison, Anita Notenboom, Dave Saunders, Gwyn Shackleton, John Spalding, Jackie Stansfield,
Helga Van De Kar and Jerry Whelan.

Additional thanks are due to Polar Music, Bocu Music and Polygram International.

For more information on ABBA write to the following addresses enclosing two International Reply Coupons:
ABBA Information, Century 22 Limited, PO Box 1326, Iver, Bucks SL0 0PP UK and
Agnetha, Benny, Björn, Frida Fan Club, PO Box 3079, 4700 AB Roosendaal, Holland.

When I first met ABBA almost two decades ago, nobody even dreamed of the incredible international fame that they would go on to achieve. It was an achievement based on talent, hard work and a sprinkling of good fortune – so easy to understand with hindsight, but impossible to have anticipated.

In the Sixties and early Seventies Björn and Benny were already enjoying a lot of local success; Benny with the Hep Stars (who were often described as the 'Swedish Beatles') and Björn with the Hootenanny Singers, while Agnetha and Anni-Frid were both pursuing successful solo careers. Despite their increasing fame in Sweden and the rest of Scandinavia, the rest of the world had never heard of them, and there was no reason to suppose that would change.

The in-depth story of how ABBA came about is detailed in this book. However, it's common knowledge that love was a significant factor in the birth of ABBA – the boys' love for Agnetha and Anni-Frid, and their love of writing songs together. Then they were privileged to win the Eurovision Song Contest back in 1974, and soon after that, their music was being heard and enjoyed all over the world – which was fantastic! It was the best thing that could possibly have happened, especially because they were from Sweden, rather than from Britain or America, the two countries that dominated popular music throughout the world before ABBA (and seem to have resumed that domination today). Perhaps that was ABBA's greatest achievement – loosening the grip of the English-speaking nations on the world's charts, even if it was only for a decade.

Flying high on the wings of fame and success for those ten years, we all had many happy times together, as well as some sad times and some really crazy times, but obviously, and for various reasons which are suggested in this book, it couldn't last forever. Since then all four group members have moved on to new challenges, fortunately still involved with music, which after all was the reason they first got together. While Frida and Agnetha embarked on separate solo careers, Björn and Benny continued to work together, doing what they know and love best – creating and making music; in particular, working with Tim Rice on the *Chess* musical.

All concerned are very pleased to see that there has been a recent resurgence of interest in the music thanks to Erasure's brilliant 'ABBA-esque' EP and those hilarious people, Björn Again, not to mention the unbelievable world-wide success of the Greatest Hits in 'ABBA Gold'. It's especially gratifying to realise that the music is now providing a lot of pleasure for a whole new generation, some of whom weren't even born when ABBA won the Eurovision Song Contest.

This book is a detailed account of their careers before, during and after ABBA. It's packed with memories for me and them alike – like a set of diaries – and I hope that ABBA fans both old and new will find it interesting and enjoyable.

John Spalding
Bocu Music

London, January 1993

ABBA are widely considered to be a Swedish group, and it's difficult to deny that they could be anything else. However, the first member of the group to make an appearance, Anni-Frid Synni Lyngstad, was actually born in Norway, near the large town of Narvik, on November 15th, 1945. This was wartime, Norway was occupied by the German army, and naturally most Norwegians were unhappy about the unwelcome guests running their country. Of course, it would be wrong to generalise about every member of the German race – while no doubt many of them were Nazis, quite a number probably felt just as unhappy about what they were doing to the innocent people of Norway as the Norwegians themselves.

Such a man was Alfred Haase, who became very friendly with a 19 year old local girl, Synni Lyngstad. Their relationship soon developed into love, which was something that the vast majority of Synni's friends and relations found quite unspeakably wrong, and the girl found herself ostracised. At the end of the war, Alfred was returned to Germany, promising to return to Narvik to marry Synni as soon as possible. He was apparently unaware that she was expecting his child, and some time after he left Norway, Anni-Frid was born. Synni Lyngstad was forced to continue her lonely life with a baby to support. She looked forward to the return of her lover, but after nearly two years the loneliness became impossible to endure, and despair replaced eager anticipation. At the age of 21, Synni Lyngstad died, alone and unhappy.

Synni's mother then had to decide what would be best for her infant grand-daughter, and as the vast majority of people she knew were aware that Anni-Frid had been born out of wedlock, and of a German father, she made the decision to move away from Narvik, across the border into Sweden, where no-one would have any idea of her origins. Thus, in 1947, Anni-Frid began a new childhood, finally settling in the district of Eskilstuna, less than a hundred miles from Stockholm, after she and her grandmother had travelled around Sweden for several years, earning enough to eat from the grandmother's work as a seamstress.

It was her grandmother who first encouraged Anni-Frid to sing, teaching her traditional Scandinavian folk songs even before the child was ten years old, which was about the time when the future member of ABBA first began to sing in public. One of her first performances was at a soirée organised by the local Red Cross when Anni-Frid was only eleven, and by the time she was 13, she was singing professionally with a dance band in an Eskilstuna restaurant, although she found it necessary to lie about her age, as she was three years below the permitted legal limit.

ANNI-FRID LYNGSTAD

(Top) From the cover of her solo album 'Frida Ensam' released in 1976
(Below) Frida aged eleven

After that, Anni-Frid began to sing with a big band led by one Bengt Sandlund, where most of the material verged on jazz, the first music at which she excelled. Another member of the Sandlund band was bass player Ragnar Frederiksson, and eventually he and Anni-Frid decided to start their own band, the Anni-Frid Four, who became a major attraction in Eskilstuna during the first half of the 1960s. During this time, Anni-Frid and Ragnar became lovers, eventually marrying, and producing two children, Hans, born on January 26th, 1963, and Liselotte, born on February 25th, 1967.

At this point, Anni-Frid seemed to have a fairly ordinary future mapped out, primarily as a wife and mother, although a certain amount of singing in the evenings provided a contrast. However, this life failed to satisfy her ambitions, and she began to enter – and win – a series of local talent contests, which culminated in *New Faces,* a national competition organised by a children's charity. Anni-Frid won her class in the competition, singing a ballad titled 'A Day Off', and after the contest was surprised to find that part of her prize was to appear on a popular TV chat show, *Hyland's Corner.*

The date of the contest was September 3rd, 1967 – a day most Swedish people remember as the great changeover, when traffic in their country converted from the traditional British mode of driving on the left to the internationally accepted right hand side of the road, but it was also the date of the television debut of one of the biggest stars to emerge from Sweden...

It became obvious that if Anni-Frid wanted to take advantage of the recording opportunities that were being offered to her, she would have to move to Stockholm, the centre of Sweden's music industry. Before the inevitable happened, she made an album and a series of singles for the Swedish EMI label, spending many months touring in cabaret and on the Swedish public park circuit. After leaving her family, Frida based herself in the Swedish capital, and it was while appearing in nightclubs in a show starring one Charlie Norman that she met Benny Andersson for the first time; Norman's show was playing one night spot in Malmo, while Benny was working with his group, The Hep Stars, at another. After this initial meeting, they often ran across each other as fellow celebrities of the pop world and, Anni-Frid's marriage having dissolved by this time, she and Benny eventually became more than just good friends.

(Top) A compilation LP of Anni-Frid's solo work including tracks recorded between 1967 and 1971
(Below) Abba in 1978

Björn Christian Ulvaeus was born in the Swedish seaside town of Gothenburg on April 25th, 1945, and moved with his family to the town of Vastervik, somewhat south of Stockholm and on the east coast of Sweden, in 1951. No doubt spurred on by his music-loving mother, Björn was given his first guitar at the age of eleven, and immediately began to play primitive versions of the simple skiffle hits which were popular at the time in Europe, graduating from that to the next British popular music craze, traditional (or Dixieland) jazz.

The first real group Björn joined was the West Bay Singers, 'West Bay' being the English translation of Vastervik. The group was formed at the school attended by Björn and his three colleagues, and was enthusiastically patronised by their art teacher, who himself was very interested in folk songs. Modelling themselves on popular contemporary American folk groups, principally The Kingston Trio, they played locally for the most part, their studies preventing them from venturing too far afield. However, during the summer of 1963, they borrowed an ancient Volvo, with a view to exploring Europe. Although still amateurs, they decided to take their instruments with them, and were able to earn a little extra spending money from the entertainment they provided.

On their return to Sweden, the group found that Björn's mother had entered them for a national talent contest sponsored by Swedish Radio. Ironically, another of the performers who had entered the competition was Anni-Frid Lyngstad...

The competition was to be the first contact between a future member of ABBA and the man who helped to pilot them to international stardom, Stig Anderson. In 1963, Stig had just formed Polar Music with a noted talent scout named Bengt Bernhag, and both Bengt and Stig were attracted by the name of the West Bay Singers, which was mentioned in a small article in a daily newspaper. Polar were on the look-out for a Swedish folk group who sang in Swedish, as the majority of performers at that time sang in English, although for the most part rather unconvincingly. Before the contest took place, they contacted the group from Vastervik, asking to hear a demonstration tape. As luck would have it, the West Bay Singers had already recorded a tape at a local radio station, which was of far better quality than the majority of test recordings, and when they sent it to Polar, Stig and Bengt were sufficiently impressed to invite the group to Stockholm for a formal audition.

Despite the fact that Polar had originally been interested in a group who sang in Swedish, the demonstration tape had been misleading: although not all their repertoire was performed in English, that was the language the West Bay Singers chiefly used, and

BJÖRN ULVÆUS

(Top) "Anyone For Croquet?"
– Björn aged twelve
(Bottom) The three-piece
Hootennany Singers, shortly
before Björn left in 1970

Stig and Bengt had to persuade them to perform a Swedish folk song both for their audition and in the talent contest. After some deliberation, they agreed, only to find that they were the only act of the twenty in the contest singing in Swedish. By this time, they had also been persuaded by Stig and Bengt to change their name to The Hootenanny Singers, which was a very American sounding name, a hootenanny being the term used to describe a folk music get-together.

The first single they released, and the song with which they won the contest, became an immediate hit, the first for Polar Records. However, the group still had to complete their education, and it wasn't until they had taken (and passed) their final examinations in the spring of 1964 that they felt ready to turn professional.

During the next two years, The Hootenanny Singers built a substantial following, touring around Sweden and frequently appearing on radio and television. They even had records released in Britain and America under the name of the Northern Lights, and scored a hit in South Africa with their single, 'No Time'. However, their career was due to meet a stumbling block: in Sweden, everyone leaving school was obliged to undergo a certain amount of military training, and by 1966, the authorities were growing impatient for the enlistment of The Hootenanny Singers. Fearing the worst, Björn and two other members of the group reported for training in the Life Guards, but found that the military authorities were far more understanding than they had expected. They were granted leave to continue their musical activities alongside their army training, and during 1967, the group scored their biggest hit up to that point with a Swedish language version of 'Green, Green Grass of Home', which Tom Jones had taken to enormous international success just a few months before.

After completing their national service, the members of The Hootenanny Singers decided to complete their education at University. While the other three went to Gothenburg, Björn enrolled at Stockholm University, and alongside his academic studies, began to learn more about the music business by working in the offices of Polar Music. This was also the time when he began to compose his own songs, although they were inevitably somewhat inferior to the material he would later help to write for ABBA. Soon the projected University studies were forgotten, as Björn found himself increasingly beguiled by the opportunities he saw in the field of music. One of the deciding factors was his growing friendship with Benny Andersson; back in 1966, when The Hootenanny Singers had been playing a concert in the Swedish town of Linkoping, Björn had met a group called The Hep Stars, who were also gigging in the town. This was his introduction to Benny, who, as their keyboard player, certainly seemed to be making a good living from full time music. Three months later, the two met again, and, on the spur of the moment, decided to write a song together, 'Isn't It Easy To Say', which was later recorded by The Hep Stars, who were one of the biggest groups in Scandinavia at the time.

By 1967, as well as recording with The Hootenanny Singers, Björn had also begun to make solo records, such as Swedish versions of American hits like 'Honey' and 'Harper Valley P.T.A.', using his own songs as B sides. In this manner, Björn continued almost until the end of the 1960s, by which time he was becoming less and less interested in the cultured folk music of The Hootenanny Singers, and leaning further towards pop and rock music. When Benny invited him to deputise on a Hep Stars tour for the group's guitarist, Janne Frick, who had failed to return from a Spanish holiday, Björn was only too eager to oblige. This was the start of a relationship, on both personal and professional levels, which would become world famous...

(Below) Björn and Benny with two of the Hootenanny Singers

BENNY ANDERSSON

Without any doubt, the most famous of the pre-ABBA quartet was Goran Bror Benny Andersson, who was born in a Stockholm suburb on December 16th, 1946. Both his father and grandfather enjoyed making music, and the six year old Benny was already vitally interested in music himself when he was given his first instrument, an accordion. He graduated to the piano at the age of ten, but from that day to this, has rarely been interested in learning to play musical instruments formally – Benny seems able to play a tune on any instrument, purely instinctively.

During his early teenage years, Benny began to perform at youth clubs, sometimes providing the backing for a girl singer, Christina Gronvall. The two were soon inseparable, and became engaged when they were both still only 15 years old. They never actually married, but their relationship produced two children, Peter, who was born on August 20th, 1963, and Helene, who appeared on June 25th, 1965. Perhaps the reason they never married was due to Benny's involvement in music, which started almost as soon as he left school. His first job was as a janitor in the engineering works run by his father, but every evening saw Benny making music, and eventually he joined a local group called Elverkerts Spelmanslag. By pure chance, this group led to Benny finding much greater fame; Elverkerts normally played gigs only a short distance from where the members of the group lived, but on one occasion during the early 1960s, they were booked to appear some distance away, which meant that they required transport to ferry themselves and their instruments to the gig. The only person they could think of who might be able to help them was Svenne Hedlund, lead singer of an up and coming group called The Hep Stars. Svenne had nothing else to do that night, and so was quite pleased to help. He watched the group, and was apparently impressed by Benny's expertise as an organ player, but thought little more about it. However, a few weeks later The Hep Stars' organist, Hans Ostlund, fell out with the others and a replacement was needed urgently. Svenne immediately thought of Benny, took the rest of the group to see him play with Elverkerts at a local restaurant, and offered him Ostlund's place in the group.

In October 1964, Benny joined The Hep Stars, who were at the time a fairly well-known, although not too successful group in Sweden. They had released a record, but it had failed to capture the public's imagination, and in the final months of 1964, the group went back into the recording studio, this time with Benny as keyboard player. Among the songs they recorded were 'Tribute To Buddy Holly', 'Farmer John' and 'Cadillac', all very much in the vein of the British beat boom which The Beatles were concurrently spearheading. When they got the chance to play 'Cadillac' on television during the first weeks

(Above) The Hep Stars in 1966
(Below) A pre-teen Benny with his accordion

of 1965, The Hep Stars produced an uninhibited performance which brought them immediate fame, although it was basically a question of behaving in the same way as their British contemporaries, moving around the stage and climbing on their amplifiers. The Hep Stars had arrived at exactly the right time; with a repertoire consisting solely of American songs, and a fascination with the works of American rock'n'rollers like Chuck Berry and The Beach Boys, the group became huge stars almost overnight, and before long, their singles filled three of the top four places in the Swedish chart.

By 1965, Benny had started to write some original material for the group, and several of his songs became hits, including 'No Response', 'Wedding' (which he co-wrote with Svenne Hedlund) and 'Sunny Girl'. The Hep Stars grew bigger and bigger, becoming the Swedish equivalent of The Beatles and ironically, making many of the same mistakes which the quartet from Liverpool would later regret. They sold records in prodigious quantities, enough to be awarded eight gold discs, but almost totally failed to ensure that the fortunes they earned were invested to protect their futures. Among numerous financial disasters, one of their biggest mistakes was the decision to make a feature film, *Habari-Safari*. This involved the whole group, plus numerous technicians, travelling to Africa for two weeks, but unfortunately, due to the fact that the script for the film had not been written in advance, very little usable footage resulted from the trip, despite the enormous amount of money it had cost.

Ultimately, their biggest mistake was failing to pay income tax on their earnings: when the Swedish Inland Revenue caught up with them at the end of 1967, they were presented with a bill for the equivalent of £100,000. Six months later, the group's production company, Hep House, an organisation apparently similar to Apple Corps, the company launched by The Beatles, went into liquidation with huge debts, and for the next two years or so, they were compelled to work as hard as they could to pay off the taxman.

During 1969, The Hep Stars decided to split into two separate camps. Three members of the group retained the name 'Hep Stars', while Benny and Svenne Hedlund decided to work with Svenne's American wife, Charlotte Walker. She had achieved fame herself during the early 1960s as a member of The Sherrys, an all-girl quartet who had scored a US hit with a song titled 'Pop-Pop-Pop-Pie'. Of course, some time before he left The Hep Stars, Benny had come into contact with Björn Ulvaeus, but perhaps more importantly from a personal point of view, he had broken up with his fiancée, the mother of his two children, during 1966. Benny seems to have had no steady girl friend for some time after that, his relationships seeming to have been rather transient and casual until he met Anni-Frid Lyngstad during 1970, when they were booked on the same radio quiz show. From that point on, their romance blossomed...

(Bottom) An early Hep Stars LP with Benny pictured top left

The youngest member of ABBA, Agnetha Ase Fältskog, was born in the south of Sweden, in the town of Jonkoping, on April 5th, 1950. Her father was an enthusiastic supporter of amateur dramatics, and used to write sketches and organise local productions, often performing in them himself. He was keen that his daughter should have a theatrical grounding, and by the time she was six, Agnetha had appeared on stage before an audience of elderly people for whom Mr. Fältskog had devised a Christmas entertainment. This would not lead to anything exceptionally exciting for Agnetha – the only thing that most observers seem to recall of the event is that halfway through, the elastic in Agnetha's pants gave way, reducing the audience to hysteria...

This set-back did not prevent her pursuing a musical education, learning both piano and accordion at an early age. Her progress continued through the early part of her teenage years, and at the age of 15, Agnetha, who idolised the American singer Connie Francis, was singing regularly with a dance band in Jonkoping, and also making guest appearances with other bands. This led to her attracting the attention of a record company talent scout named Little Gerhard, who had continued to use his stage name even after giving up performing for a less glamorous job in the pop music business. Originally, Gerhard had been sent the tape by one of his distant relatives, whose singing covered most of the tape, but it was Agnetha's far less prominent vocals which impressed Gerhard enough to request a full audition tape of the 17 year old girl.

Agnetha sent him a recording of a song she had written while trying to console herself over the loss of a boyfriend, 'I Was So In Love'. Little Gerhard was so impressed that he immediately invited her to Stockholm to record the song: within weeks, Agnetha had signed to the CBS-Cupol record label, and her record was topping the Swedish chart in early 1968.

The hits continued throughout the late 1960s, and it was also during this time that Agnetha became engaged to a German songwriter/producer named Dieter Zimmerman, but the romance was shortlived. Some of the songs she recorded attracted controversy – 'Gypsy Friend', which she recorded in 1969 (and for which she wrote the music, but not the lyrics), was called "tasteless" by Swedish newspapers, as a national debate about gypsies was taking place at the time of the record's release, although the connection between the song and the debate was purely coincidental. Another song, 'If Tears Were Gold', provoked accusations from a Danish bandleader who claimed that Agnetha had stolen the melody from a song he had written, and which he had featured during a tour of

AGNETHA FÄLTSKOG

Sweden. He tried to sue her for plagiarism, but his case lost much of its impetus when it was disclosed that his Swedish tour had taken place in 1950, the year that Agnetha was born. A child prodigy she may have been, but to have stolen a tune before she was a year old...

By the end of the Sixties, Agnetha had become a big star in Sweden, with numerous hit records to her credit, but because of the pressures and demands of the music business, she seems to have found it difficult to form a steady romantic relationship. However, that aspect of her life was to change during the summer of 1969, when she met Björn Ulvaeus after both were booked to appear on a Swedish television show. They were immediately attracted to each other, and by the next year had become engaged. The pieces of the ABBA jigsaw were beginning to fall into place...

(Top) Agnetha in 1963, aged thirteen
(Right) Agnetha and Björn on their wedding day
(Below Left) Agnetha's first solo album, released in 1968
(Bottom Right) Agnetha and Björn with their first child Linda

1969-72

THE FORMATIVE YEARS

By the end of the 1960s, Benny and Björn had formalised their professional relationship, setting up their own company, Union Songs, in partnership with Stig Anderson, who by this time was eager for them to write songs in English, as he could see that his protégés represented the biggest chance thus far for a Swedish act to achieve worldwide fame. By 1970, as well as songs like 'Isn't It Easy To Say' and 'A Flower In My Garden', both of which had been recorded by The Hep Stars, the duo had recorded and released a single, 'She's My Kind Of Girl', which later became an enormous hit in Japan, selling half a million copies in 1972. In fact, the song had been written several years earlier and was only released after a chance hearing by a Japanese music publisher. Added to this was an album by Björn and Benny, 'Lycka' (the title means happiness), to which Stig Anderson contributed lyrics to the title track – one of the earliest collaborations of the trio of Stig, Björn and Benny, which would later be responsible for several international smash hits. Stig was already a pastmaster at creating lyrics, having written more than 2,000 songs during the 1960s and early 1970s, which made him Scandinavia's best known lyricist during this period.

Shortly before the end of 1969, the personal lives of the future members of ABBA began to solidify: in August, 1969, Benny and Anni-Frid became engaged, and two months later, Björn and Agnetha followed suit... but it was still to be some time before the foursome would decide to work together. Benny and Björn obviously displayed an interest in the careers of their fiancées, and Benny produced an LP for Anni-Frid, which was released by EMI Records in Sweden.

By 1970, Benny and Anni-Frid were living together, as were Björn and Agnetha, and the girls were pursuing separate careers, while Benny and Björn were operating as a duo. It was a fairly obvious move for the four to think about performing together, and the first occasion on which they were able to do so occured when Björn and Benny were booked

to appear at a restaurant in Gothenburg during November, 1970. Neither Anni-Frid nor Agnetha were working that evening, so it was decided that they would help out their boyfriends. Hurriedly, an act was devised and the untried group took the stage as Festfolk, which, depending on the way it's spelt, can mean either 'party people' or 'engaged couples'.

This historic event, the first appearance of ABBA (although not under that name) was apparently a total disaster – the carefully co-ordinated show, designed to appeal to a restaurant audience, was completely inappropriate, because none of the performers were very interested in the songs they were singing. ABBA's career was nearly finished, several years before it had even started.

THE NAME OF FAME

During 1971, Björn and Benny concentrated on songwriting, one of their bigger successes being with 'Language Of Love', a song with lyrics by Stig which they entered for a song festival in Malaga, where it was placed sixth. Despite this accolade, they were more encouraged when French actress/singer Françoise Hardy subsequently recorded the song. Anni-Frid went back to her solo career, acting in a theatrical revue, and singing one of the songs entered for the Swedish heat of the Eurovision Song Contest. It was some way from winning, so Anni-Frid reverted to her recording career, releasing another LP. Agnetha also tried her hand at theatrics, playing Mary Magdalene in a Swedish production of the Tim Rice/Andrew Lloyd Webber rock opera, *Jesus Christ Superstar*. Following this she recorded a song from the show, 'I Don't Know How To Love Him', which became a huge hit. Agnetha had only taken the part at Björn's suggestion, and it was again Björn who correctly predicted that 'Our Earth Is Wonderful', a song she had written, would be a massive hit for her later that same year.

In the summer of 1971, Benny, Björn and Agnetha formed a trio to perform at concerts held in Swedish public parks, generally known as the 'folkpark' circuit. For some months now, Agnetha and Björn, having decided to get married, had been looking for a suitably romantic church in which to conduct their wedding ceremony, and during the tour, they found a very old Gothic church in the village of Verum, near Skane in the south of Sweden, which they felt would be perfect for their requirements. However, a minor snag occurred when they contacted the local clergyman. When he asked their professions, Björn and Agnetha replied 'Artists', but the clergyman misheard, thinking they had said 'Atheists', and at first refused to marry the couple. The misunderstanding was soon cleared up, and on July 7th, 1971, Agnetha arrived at the ancient church in an open carriage drawn by a team of white horses, having driven through a crowd of more than 3,000 people. As she entered the church with Björn, the 'Wedding March' was played by Benny on the church organ, and he followed it with 'Wedding', the song he had co-written with Svenne Hedlund for The Hep Stars.

The day was a great success, despite the fact that in the confusion caused by the unexpected crowds, Agnetha was slightly injured when a police horse stepped on her foot, and the happy couple left for a short honeymoon before restarting their folkpark tour. However, it wasn't long before a darker cloud permeated the proceedings, as news came from Stockholm that Bengt Bernhag, Stig Anderson's partner, and the man who with Stig had originally discovered Björn, had committed suicide on the day of the wedding. Bengt had for some time suffered from colitis, which had affected his confidence to the point where he rarely ventured from his home, and almost never allowed himself to be seen in public. Bengt had been invited to the wedding, of course, but his disability had caused him to refuse the invitation, and it was generally assumed that he decided to take his own life in a severe fit of depression at not being able to enjoy Björn and Agnetha's big day.

Bengt's death was a major tragedy, but from it came another major step on the road which would lead to the formation of ABBA. Stig Anderson, having lost his partner, needed a new producer and business associate, a position which he offered to Björn. Initially, Björn refused, saying he wouldn't do it unless Benny worked with him,

(Top) The first ABBA connected chart record in the United States, 'People Need Love'

whereupon Stig indicated that he couldn't afford to pay salaries to two producers. It didn't take long before Björn agreed that he and Benny would share a single salary, and one of their first jobs for Polar Music was to produce the first LP by Ted Gardestad, an artist in whose career Benny, Björn and Stig continued to take considerable interest for several subsequent years.

Before the end of 1971, Benny, Björn, Agnetha and Anni-Frid made another abortive attempt to combine their talents into a single stage act. Once again, Gothenburg was chosen to stage their 'supersession', and although the response was somewhat better than that which greeted their first attempt, things still weren't working as they should. A further barrier on the road towards ABBA was constructed by Stig Anderson, although quite unwittingly: Björn and Agnetha decided to record a song together describing their romance, 'This Is The Way Love Starts', but because Agnetha was signed to CBS-Cupol Records, this had to be the label on which the track was released. Björn, of course, was signed to Polar Records, and Stig quite reasonably refused to allow his artist to record for another label. This stalemate led to the record's release being delayed for some time...

FIRST SIGNS OF SUCCESS

1972 saw the first records featuring all four members of ABBA together, although the name ABBA was not used on them. First came 'She's My Kind Of Girl', which, as already mentioned, was a big hit in Japan for Björn and Benny. Both Agnetha and Anni-Frid were featured on the record, but were not credited on the label. Björn and Benny also scored their first minor Eurovision success with a song they and Stig wrote for Lena Andersson, a Swedish singer described as a cross between Judy Collins and Joan Baez. The song, 'Better To Have Loved', was placed third in the Swedish Eurovision heat, but when released commercially, it reached Number One in Sweden, which was certainly some consolation. The success of 'She's My Kind Of Girl', meanwhile, had led to an invitation for Björn and Benny to submit an entry for a Japanese Song Festival, held in Tokyo. They took their 'other halves' with them, and the song performed by the quartet, Santa Rosa, was very well received.

Back in Sweden, Björn and Benny recorded a new single, 'People Need Love', with 'Merry Go Round' as its flipside. Once again, Agnetha and Anni-Frid helped them in the recording studio, and it was obvious that the girls would have to be mentioned on the record's label because their voices were so prominent. At first, Stig Anderson refused to credit them, quite naturally suggesting that Björn, Benny, Agnetha and Frida was far too unwieldy a name, but Björn and Benny insisted that it was released using all four names, and Stig eventually capitulated. The record was a big hit all over Scandinavia, reaching No.2 in Sweden, and also became the first single by the quartet to be released in the USA, where it was credited to Björn and Benny with Svenska Flicka when it emerged on Playboy Records, the label associated with the famous *Playboy* magazine. The single was making promising strides towards the US Top 100 when Playboy experienced problems in finding a distributor able to keep up with demand for the record. As a result, Björn and Benny were deprived of what looked like a certain hit. Even so, the record's peak just outside the all-important Top 100 at No.115 was apparently the highest US chart position ever reached by a Swedish record up to that point.

At the end of 1972, after a year when both 'People Need Love' and its follow up, 'He Is Your Brother', had been sizeable hits in Sweden, the songwriting trio of Björn, Benny and Stig were approached by the Swedish Broadcasting Company, who invited them to submit an entry for the Swedish heat of the Eurovision Song Contest. And that's where the story of ABBA really starts...

(Below) Receiving the Carl Allen Award from Princess Margaret

(Right) The first ABBA LP

1973
RING RING –
WRONG
NUMBER
FOR
EUROVISION

The start of 1973 saw Björn Ulvaeus, Benny Andersson and Stig Anderson ensconced on the small island where each of them maintained a holiday home, working hard to produce a song which would win the Swedish heat of the Eurovision Song Contest, and would thus represent their country in the Eurovision final which was due to be held in Luxembourg later that year. Benny and Björn slaved over the music, aiming towards a ringing sound like a peal of bells, while Stig iced the cake with lyrics and a perfectly appropriate title, 'Ring Ring'. After their near miss as composers the previous year, it was a foregone conclusion that the song would be performed by Björn, Benny, Agnetha & Anni-Frid, and Björn and Benny spent long hours in the recording studio with Michael Tretow, an engineer whom they had first met back in 1970, when he was the junior engineer at Metronome Studios working on the 'Lycka' album. By the time of the sessions for 'Ring Ring', Micke (as he is known) was permanently attached to Polar Music, with special responsibilities for engineering recordings by Björn and Benny and the girls, and it was he who helped to construct the vitally important instrumental backing for the Eurovision entry.

The Swedish heat was held in Stockholm on February 10th, 1973, and this introduced another complication for the quartet. Agnetha was nearing the end of her pregnancy, and her doctor had forecast that the baby was due on, or very close to, the date of the contest. From one point of view, it was almost an advantage, as a great deal of publicity both for the contest and the group could be easily acquired in the form of photographs of a beaming Agnetha, obviously gleefully anticipating motherhood, but what would happen if she found herself in hospital on the day of the contest? In order to cover all possibilities, Anni-Frid learned all the female vocal parts of the song, so that it would be possible for her to perform it without Agnetha, but in the event, this insurance was unnecessary, as the child had still shown no signs of making an appearance by the time the contest got underway.

Björn, Benny, Agnetha and Anni-Frid performed splendidly, earning a riotous reception from the audience, and it seemed as though their victory was assured. Unfortunately for them, however, the winners of the contest were not judged on the basis of the audience's reaction, but by a panel of so-called experts, who ignored the response of the crowd and instead selected another song as the Swedish Eurovision entry for 1973. This, of course, was bitterly disappointing for Björn, Benny and Stig, whose song had once again been placed third. The difference from their previous third place with Lena Andersson's 'Better To Have Loved' was that this time, public opinion was so enraged that the experts had chosen another song instead of 'Ring Ring' that a major controversy developed,

especially after a Stockholm evening paper conducted a telephone poll which proved quite conclusively that a large majority of ordinary people felt that the song which had been chosen was the wrong one to represent Sweden, a country which had never won the Eurovision Contest since it had started in 1956. The result of this furore was that in future years, the panel of 'experts' was replaced by a cross-section of the general public.

Subsequently, each of those involved in the creation of 'Ring Ring' has admitted that, in many ways, the song's failure to become the Swedish entry for the 1973 Eurovision Contest was a blessing in disguise, since it was necessary preparation for their future triumphs. Björn, Benny, Agnetha and Anni-Frid had been such hot favourites to win the Swedish heat of the contest that Stig Anderson had arranged for 'Ring Ring' to be recorded not only in Swedish, but also in German, Spanish and English – which eventually resulted in ABBA's first British release, although not before that long and unwieldy title of Björn, Benny, Anna and Frida (which was the first attempt at shortening the name) had been reduced to the simpler and much more memorable ABBA.

The first significant event after the 'Ring Ring' fiasco was the arrival, on February 23rd, 1973, of Elin Linda Ulvaeus, Agnetha and Björn's first child. For much of the next decade, Agnetha and her daughter were almost inseparable, although it was undoubtedly very difficult for Agnetha to fulfil her commitments to both daughter and career at certain busy times. Nevertheless, history proves that she managed the task very well. At the tender age of four days, Linda was presented to the Swedish press in the Stockholm hospital where she was born. In many ways, this press conference was another master stroke: despite their failure in the contest, 'Ring Ring', which had been released as a single in Sweden, was achieving maximum publicity, and as Björn later noted, it was highly unlikely that the child would suffer any ill effects from all the fuss, and in fact would be able to look back on a superb photographic record of the event.

'Ring Ring' became an enormous success: the Swedish version of the song topped the charts in Norway, Denmark and Finland, while the English version reached Number One in Australia, Holland, Belgium and South Africa. This was in addition to its record beating success at home in Sweden, where the Swedish language version of 'Ring Ring' was Number One, the English version No.2, and the 'Ring Ring' LP No.3! Despite all the clamour, Stig Anderson was finding it extremely difficult to get the record released in Britain, where three major companies turned it down. Still, it was just as important to maintain the success that Björn, Benny, Agnetha and Anni-Frid had achieved elsewhere, and the quartet returned to the studio to record their follow up single, 'Love Isn't Easy'.

By the time this was released during the second half of 1973, Stig found himself continually talking to journalists about the foursome he looked after, and before long, had begun to refer to the group as ABBA, using the initial letters of their first names. It wasn't long before the Swedish press picked up on the name and one Gothenburg newspaper ran a poll to discover what their readers felt about the group being known by this new title. There were other suggestions, of course, but apparently eighty per cent of those who replied felt that ABBA was a particularly appropriate name, and ABBA is what it became and remained.

(Below) Gentlemen prefer Blondes!
Agnetha jokes with a posse of admirers

A small initial problem was that a well-known Swedish fish canning company was also known as ABBA. Stig was initially concerned that he might be prevented from using the name, but was relieved to discover that the owners of the canning firm were very happy to share it, although they indicated that they would be far less pleased if the group indulged in any kind of unpleasant behaviour which might reflect badly on their products. Events proved that such a warning really wasn't at all necessary, although they weren't to know that at the time...

28

October 12th, 1973
RING RING/ROCK'N ROLL BAND (Epic EPC 1793)

After being turned down by at least three British record companies, Stig Anderson finally convinced Epic Records, part of the CBS 'family', to release the English version of 'Ring Ring', which thus became the first ABBA record issued in Britain. While the tune was unchanged from the original Swedish version, veteran American hitmaker Neil Sedaka and his songwriting partner of the time, Phil Cody, had been contracted to supply appropriate English lyrics.

Despite all these special arrangements, 'Ring Ring' was a resounding flop in Britain, which should really have come as no surprise; after all, the group were almost completely unknown in the British Isles, and it seems unlikely that more than a handful of people ever heard the record at the time, and then probably by accident rather than design. Added to this, Epic were the fourth company to be offered the record, and although they eventually agreed to release it, their suspicions about its lack of hit potential may have resulted in a less than ardent promotional campaign.

It should also be noted that, compared to ABBA's later recordings, 'Ring Ring' can only be rated as an average song; the Sedaka/Cody lyrics, while eminently suitable for Eurovision, seem rather trite, and it's difficult to understand why Benny, Björn and Stig had so little faith in their own lyrical ability, especially as 'Rock'n' Roll Band', written by Björn and Benny without outside help, has perfectly adequate lyrics, although once again, they're part of a song which is hardly special. Even so, 'Rock'n' Roll Band' possesses a mark of distinction, in that it was one of the most difficult ABBA recordings to acquire, not having been included on a British LP until 1992. Interestingly enough, 'Ring Ring' was a hit in Ireland – but not for ABBA. The song was covered by an Irish group called The Others, who rode their version into the Top 20.

(Below) ABBA take to the water, 1973

ABBA with Sven-Olof Waldoff in Brighton for Eurovision

1974
HOME WIN FOR WATERLOO – NOW FOR EUROPE

Disappointed by the failure of 'Ring Ring' in Eurovision terms, but greatly consoled by its significant chart position throughout much of Europe, ABBA spent much of the second half of 1973 touring the Swedish folkparks, after which Benny, Björn and Stig Anderson began to make preparations for their next assault on the international rock scene – the 1974 Eurovision Contest. This time, they were determined to represent Sweden, particularly as the jury who would choose the national entry were no longer so-called experts, but normal ordinary people who would be far more representative of the feelings of the Swedish population as a whole.

ABBA's run up to Eurovision actually started almost six months before the contest was due to take place. By November 1973, Stig Anderson had ascertained that most music business people around Europe felt that the 1974 Eurovision winner would be a fairly fast-paced song, as several ballads had won the competition in previous years. With this in mind, Benny and Björn set about writing a bouncy, catchy tune which would capture their audience's imagination, without being as trivial as most Eurovision fare. After several weeks of experiment, during which they arrived at a melody and musical arrangement which seemed appropriate, they had to choose a theme, a title and suitable lyrics for their song. In fact, the title came first; a world-wide pop hit, which was what they were aiming for, needed a title which was easily recognisable in Spain, in Japan, in Eastern European countries, in fact, in every country where the record would be released.

Stig, who made himself responsible for selecting the all-important title, knew that it must be easily pronounceable by people who spoke no English, and that its meaning must be clear all over the world. His first thoughts revolved around the title 'Honey Pie', but

somehow this didn't seem suitable, and after more cogitation, he came up with 'Waterloo'. The next task was to write lyrics which matched the ideas suggested by the title, and these were successfully completed during the early part of 1974. Everything now seemed ready for the first hurdle, the Swedish Eurovision heat.

Then came a red herring: Björn and Benny produced another tune which sounded equally strong, although they didn't have a title for it. Stig, who was about to go on holiday to the Canary Isles, took a cassette of the new melody with him, and pondered over the problem, until finally he adopted a phrase used by everyone in the Canaries, 'Hasta Manana', which means 'see you tomorrow'. It was a perfect title for the new song, but that presented another problem – should it be 'Waterloo' or 'Hasta Manana' for Eurovision? Fortunately, another factor had to be taken into consideration: it would be better for the chosen song to involve all four members of ABBA, and 'Hasta Manana' was designed to be sung chiefly by Agnetha. So 'Waterloo' it was, and on February 9th, 1974, ABBA performed the song for the Swedish jury, who gave the song an overwhelming vote of confidence, giving it over sixty per cent of the total marks. They were in the final.

Apart from the extreme care taken in crafting the song, ABBA knew that they would enhance their chances of winning if they worked hard to polish the visual side of their act; with around three minutes to impress the Eurovision jury, nothing which might positively influence the voting should be ignored. Taking the outrageous and hugely successful Gary Glitter as their inspiration, ABBA devised clothes which would be both eye-catching and unusual, ending up with colourful costumes liberally decorated with sequins. However, their master stroke involved the conductor of the Eurovision Orchestra on the vital night, Sven-Olof Waldoff, who had coincidentally led the orchestra for Agnetha's very first record, back in 1967. To further enhance the 'Waterloo' theme, Waldoff agreed to appear in a Napoleonic outfit, complete with the general's distinctive headgear. Whatever happened, ABBA were determined that Europe should not forget their performance!

The contest was due to be held in April, but some time before, Stig began his campaign to familiarise Europe with ABBA and their song. 'Waterloo' was released in several countries some weeks before the contest, becoming a hit in some, most notably Sweden where 110,000 copies of the single were sold, together with 97,000 copies of a similarly titled album. Even if their carefully laid plans were frustrated on the night, Stig wanted to make sure that ABBA benefited from 'Waterloo', and he made a whistle-stop-tour of Europe, distributing copies of the record in specially designed publicity folders.

Anni-Frid soaking up the sun

April 1974 arrived, and ABBA made the trip to England where the contest was to be held, taking with them at least three 'good luck charms'. Agnetha had been given a stuffed toy donkey by a fan, and although it was rather large, she insisted that it accompanied her on the journey; Anni-Frid insisted on wearing a large hat at all times (although not in bed, as some comedians suggested); and Björn designed a special guitar for himself, which was not only another talisman, but an extra boost to their visual presentation, as its body was shaped like a star.

BRIGHTON BREAKTHROUGH

When they arrived in Brighton, ABBA found that they were 6-1 favourites to win the contest, perhaps because of Stig's intensive campaign, but by the day before the contest, their position had altered substantially, and England, represented by Olivia Newton-John, had emerged as new favourites, followed by the oddly-named Dutch duo of Mouth & McNeal. ABBA's odds had slipped to 20-1, and one English national newspaper printed a picture of the group, with a caption 'No-hopers who have something to sing about'. Despite this pessimistic turn of events, Stig Anderson remained convinced of ABBA's supremacy and backed them at 20-1, while Benny also felt it was worth a little flutter, although he wagered only £10 as opposed to Stig's £20...

Due to the world's political climate in 1974, it was feared that there might be some danger to certain contestants, as a result of which everything surrounding the Song

Contest was protected by a heavy blanket of security; in particular the entrants from Greece, Northern Ireland and Israel were sheltered from possible demonstration, but in the event nothing occurred to disturb the smooth running of the gala. However, even if political sabotage seemed a very remote possibility to ABBA, the rehearsals for the event pointed out unforeseen problems of a different nature; their musical backing track, which had been pre-recorded in accordance with the rules of the competition, lacked the necessary power and vitality when broadcast over the hall's PA system, and ABBA found it very discouraging when they came to sing along with it.

Fortunately, by the evening of the contest proper, April 6th, 1974, all the difficulties had been resolved, and the small audience within the Dome in Brighton, plus the estimated 500 million television viewers throughout Europe, saw ABBA deliver a faultless and magical performance, which clinched the Contest by a clear margin.

All the careful preparation had finally paid off, although one or two jarring notes occurred during the 24 hours immediately following their triumph. The first annoyance came when the group were presented with their trophy; a further prize was awarded to the composers of the winning song, and while Stig was able to walk on-stage to collect the award, over-zealous security guards made it very difficult for Benny and Björn, who had co-written 'Waterloo', to accompany him. Of course, this was a relatively minor point: the important thing was that ABBA had won...

After champagne celebrations lasting into the small hours, they retired for the night... only for Stig to be woken up by a phone call from a Swedish journalist, who asked him if he had forgotten that more than 40,000 people died at the Battle of Waterloo. Fortunately for the scribe, Stig was too ecstatic to respond unpleasantly to such a stupid question, or to another caller from Sweden who accused ABBA of plagiarism, suggesting that 'Waterloo' bore startling similarities to both 'Build Me Up Buttercup', a 1960's hit for the Foundations, and to a Tchaikovsky Piano Concerto!

After only a few hours sleep, ABBA were the guests of honour at a champagne breakfast organised by CBS/Epic Records at the Bedford Hotel in Brighton. Journalists and broadcasters from all over Europe were there, together with another CBS star act, The Wombles, and more champagne flowed, as the group were interviewed by dozens of people whom they'd never met before, and photographed by legions of cameramen. Agnetha was the only casualty of this activity – immediately after the contest she had suffered a recurrence of a throat infection which would continue to afflict her from time to time until she finally gave up smoking some time later.

The rest of the week was filled with more receptions and parties in London, plus a triumphant appearance on *Top Of The Pops*. Both Björn and Agnetha, who had previously decided that they would be getting their hair cut after Eurovision, changed their minds because they had been photographed so often! More importantly, most music critics had enjoyed ABBA's Eurovision performance immensely, feeling that as the first group ever to win it, they had brought something fresh and exciting to what was usually a fairly banal contest. "Eurovision will never be the same again" they wrote hopefully, but, almost inevitably, it reverted to its normal pattern in subsequent years.

April 5th, 1974
WATERLOO/WATCH OUT (Epic EPC 2240)

Released the day before the Eurovision Contest, this was the record which really launched the ABBA success story in Britain and America. The group set new standards of creativity and innovation in the Eurovision Contest, beating Italy's Gigliola Cinquetti (a previous Eurovision winner) into second place. By the Monday following the contest, Epic had despatched to leading record shops throughout Britain 25,000 copies of 'Waterloo', together with a specially designed poster. A week later, the single entered the British charts, reaching the Number One position by the beginning of May, and remaining there for a second week during its nine week stay in the best-selling list.

April 7th 1974 – On Brighton Beach the day after their Eurovision Victory

WATERLOO

ABBA (BJÖRN, BENNY, ANNA & FRIDA)

ABBA 26/2

'Waterloo' remains one of the finest ABBA recordings, retaining its freshness throughout the 1970s and continuing to draw an enthusiastic response at all their live concerts. 'Watch Out' was also a major progression from what little had been heard of ABBA in Britain before this time: Björn's lead vocal, set against interjections from the girls, makes the song somewhat reminiscent of 'I Can't Control Myself', a big 1966 hit for The Troggs. Like so many ABBA singles, both sides of the record seem equally strong, and either track is a perfect illustration of the group's rapidly improving prowess. 'Waterloo' became a hit in many countries around the world, and topped the charts in 14 territories. More importantly, it became ABBA's first hit in America, where it reached the Top 10 in each of the three major music trade magazines, its highest placing being at No.7 in *Billboard* magazine.

April 5th, 1974
SI (by Gigliola Cinquetti)/MEIN RUF NACH DIR (by Piera Martell); WATERLOO (by ABBA)/WONDERFUL DREAM (by Anne-Marie David) (CBS/Epic CBS/EPC 2283)

Possibly the most obscure British release to feature ABBA, this 'maxi-single EP', as it was described, is sub-titled 'The Music People At Eurovision', and collects together the three 1974 Eurovision entries licensed to the CBS group in Britain. Italy's entry was 'Si', which finished as runner up to ABBA in the contest, and was also released in an English language version titled 'Go (Before You Break My Heart)'. In this form, it became a hit in Britain, eventually reaching the Top 10 in the UK singles chart. Piera Martell was Switzerland's Eurovision entry, and perhaps the only thing that will be remembered of the lady or her song is that when she wasn't singing, Piera worked as a bricklayer! The final

track on the record, 'Wonderful Dream', was a convenient inclusion, as it was the song with which Anne-Marie David won the previous year's Eurovision contest for Luxembourg. The obscurity of this release was increased by the fact that apparently the only copies manufactured were for promotional purposes, and were given to journalists and broadcasters covering the Eurovision contest. It remains one of the very few records to feature ABBA alongside other artists, although during the mid-1970s, CBS Records were in the habit of releasing hit single compilation albums, and ABBA appeared on two of these, although they were available only for a few weeks. Their contribution to the 'Hit Sound '74' album was 'Waterloo', and 'S.O.S.' was included on the following year's 'Hit Sound '75'.

May 17th, 1974
WATERLOO (LP) (Epic EPC 80179)
Side One: WATERLOO/SITTING IN THE PALMTREE/KING KONG SONG/ HASTA MANANA/MY MAMA SAID/DANCE(WHILE THE MUSIC STILL GOES ON)
Side Two: HONEY, HONEY/WATCH OUT/WHAT ABOUT LIVINGSTONE/ GONNA SING YOU MY LOVESONG/SUZY-HANG-AROUND/ RING RING

'Waterloo' was the first ABBA album to be released in Britain (and in America), although perhaps it might never have seen the light of day had the group not won Eurovision. Not, as some critics suggested, a hastily assembled collection to cash in on the success of 'Waterloo' as a single, this well-structured album had been recorded over a period of four months, beginning in October 1973. Prior to its release, three of the 12 tracks had been issued as singles, while a fourth, 'Honey, Honey', was to make the British Top 10 later in 1974 when covered by the boy/girl duo, Sweet Dreams. Although ABBA's version of 'Honey, Honey' was never released as a single in Britain, it was issued as the follow up to 'Waterloo' in America, where it was coupled with 'Dance (While The Music Still Goes

On)' to make a rather more subdued chart impact. The latter track features Agnetha singing along with minimal orchestral backing before the rest of the group sing with her. The remaining tracks are marked by the obvious professionalism of Björn and Benny, who produced the album and co-wrote the majority of the material, sharing the remaining composing credits with Stig Anderson, with the exception of 'Ring Ring', where the Sedaka/Cody English lyric is used in conjunction with the music of the Anderson/Ulvaeus/Andersson team. Among the stand-out tracks are 'King Kong Song', which seems to owe an affectionate debt to The Beach Boys. long time favourites of Benny and Björn, 'Suzy-Hang-Around', which, apart from bearing an uncanny resemblance to the early work of The Hollies, is one of the few ABBA recordings on which Benny takes the lead vocal, and the lyrically ingenious 'What About Livingstone'. a song comparing the exploits of the African explorer to the journeys of a cosmonaut. It also seems worth noting that 'Sitting In The Palmtree' seems to be an early example of Euro-Reggae, if such a hybrid exists. 'Hasta Manana', the song which was seriously considered for Eurovision, is also included, and later became the B side of the third ABBA single released in America, the A side of which was 'Ring Ring'. The 'Waterloo' album also marks the last time that ABBA produced both Swedish and English versions of their recordings, the swan song being the title track. As Benny remarked in 1979, "Why should we bother to still record in Swedish? Everybody buys our English versions in Sweden anyway..."

One other thing – even at this early stage of their international career, Björn and Benny took care to credit the musicians who had helped them to create the unique ABBA sound. Surprisingly, the majority of the 'Waterloo' album was made with a nucleus of only five musicians – Benny on various keyboard instruments, Björn on acoustic guitar, Janne Schaffer on electric guitar, Rutger Gunnarsson on bass and Ola Brunkert on drums. A measure of the loyalty inspired by ABBA is that Ola and Rutger were still providing the group's backing on their 1979 world tour, although Janne Schaffer had by then become a well-known artist in his own right, making several jazz-influenced guitar albums.

A DIFFICULT DECISION

If the first six months of 1974 had provided enormous success for ABBA in terms of expanding their areas of influence, the second half of the year was rather less noteworthy, although Americans experienced their first taste of the group's music by way of the 'Waterloo' single and album. The single reached the Top 10, of course, while the rather less successful album peaked at around number 150. However, although the vast majority of American record buyers failed to appreciate the album, several influential critics were fulsome in their praise of ABBA. Greg Shaw, writing in *Who Put The Bomp,* called the group's music "the marriage of that long estranged couple, Rock'n'Roll and Pop," while Ken Barnes noted in *Rolling Stone* that 'Waterloo' "made button-punching on the car radio a worthwhile pastime again," and another anonymous reviewer called the album "a positive blast of inspirational music with the potential to break big – look for another supergroup."

Certainly, a good start in America, but elsewhere things were less promising, especially in Britain, and strangely enough, in Sweden. Even before they had won the Swedish Eurovision heat, ABBA had verbally agreed to play a number of concerts on the folkpark circuit during the summer of 1974. The commitment had been made in January of that year, but six months later, circumstances had altered so radically that the tour would have been a positive disadvantage. The first problem was the health of the members of the group – the day after Eurovision, Agnetha had been laid low with a throat infection, and each one of the group was showing signs of the strain of constant travelling to various European countries for interviews and television appearances. To undertake the folkpark tour would have meant losing two valuable months, one in rehearsal and one actually performing, at a time when they needed to rest, selecting only those engagements prestigious enough to aid their conquest of foreign territories. Added to this was the fact that Björn and Benny were contracted to Polar Music as producers, and during the first half of 1974, the artists for whom they were responsible, including Ted Gardestad and Lena Andersson, had been completely neglected. And then there was the question of new songs for the rapidly developing ABBA...

It was obviously a difficult decision – should they cancel the tour (which they were legally entitled to do, as no formal contracts had been signed), and concentrate instead on the more important issue of breaking through in countries like America, Japan and Australia, or should they honour their obligations and to all intents and purposes waste two crucial months, hoping that international audiences would remember them? Obviously, there could only be one answer, and despite numerous complaints from promoters who no doubt felt they were being cheated of fortunes by ABBA cancelling the tour, the group pulled out, ironically to be replaced by the Dutch duo of Mouth & McNeal, whom they had beaten into third place in the Eurovision contest. By way of consolation, ABBA planned to arrange a full European tour for the next winter...

Björn and Agnetha in rehearsal

June 21st, 1974
RING RING/WATCH OUT (Epic EPC 1793)

As 'Waterloo' dropped out of the British charts, Epic decided to re-release ABBA's first British single, although in a slightly remixed version courtesy of Paul Atkinson of the CBS International A&R Department. The changes actually made little difference, as the single was not the big hit everyone expected it to be, peaking at No.32 in the chart during a five week residency in the Top 50. Critics were divided about the record, one music paper calling it "the epitome of blandness and mediocrity" and another noting "the group confirms its ability with an attractively varied plea from Anna." In case anyone wonders who Anna is, the journalist concerned was echoing the name by which certain CBS Records staff referred to Agnetha, a name they found difficulty in pronouncing. Despite the press disagreements about the record, in fact the major reason for its lack of chart progress probably revolved around an industrial dispute which forced *Top Of The Pops* off the air on the week in which ABBA were due to appear. Rather an anti-climax after a chart topper, the re-released 'Ring Ring' still sold over 50,000 copies in Britain, over ten times as many as it had managed nine months earlier when ABBA were still virtually unknown.

Around the time when 'Ring Ring' was re-released in the UK, ABBA made their first trip to the US, where 'Waterloo' was climbing the charts. They appeared on the top rated *Mike Douglas Show*, giving many American and Canadian journalists their first chance to get to grips with what would turn out to be a new pop music phenomenon. This first North American visit was inevitably brief, as many things had to be organised back in Sweden. One of the items on their agenda was the preparation of a new stage act for the forthcoming winter tour, and both Agnetha and Anni-Frid embarked on a course of dancing lessons under the tuition of black American choreographer Graham Tainton, while Björn and Benny started thinking about new songs for inclusion in the tour and on a new album, which they hoped to complete before the end of the year. As it happened, that became impossible due to their backlog of production commitments.

The tour, ABBA's first lengthy trek around Europe, involved enormous amounts of expensive and sophisticated amplification and lighting, and to facilitate the administration and transport problems presented in moving this equipment around Europe, and also allow the touring party sufficient time to recover, it was decided to split the itinerary into three two week stages separated by rest periods. This arrangement particularly pleased Agnetha, who felt that it would be wrong to be away from her daughter Linda, at the time not yet two years old, for any longer than a few days at a time.

The first leg of the tour began in the Danish capital of Copenhagen on November 17th, 1974, and continued for the next thirteen days in West Germany, Austria and Switzerland, before ending back in West Germany at the end of the month. To call it a resounding success would not be wholly accurate: Copenhagen was the only sold-out show, everywhere else displaying varying numbers of empty seats. Hardly the most pleasant start to a tour – and the situation wasn't alleviated by ABBA's next record released in Britain...

November 29th, 1974
SO LONG/I'VE BEEN WAITING FOR YOU (Epic EPC 2848)

Apart from the original issue of 'Ring Ring', this was the only ABBA single which failed to reach the British chart; bad news, when success had been regarded as crucial by both group and record company. Historically, every previous continental European artist rising to prominence through Eurovision had been unable to follow up their initial hit, and winning Eurovision seemed to result in isolated international success rather than a long and flourishing career. ABBA had already proved that they were more than just 'one-hit-wonders' although 'Ring Ring' had been far less successful than its predecessor, but they were considerably disappointed by the chart failure of this, their third single, comprising the first two tracks released from new recording sessions undertaken since the

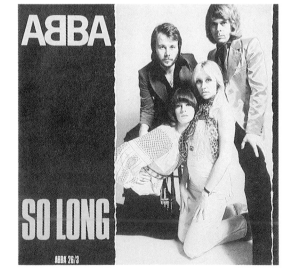

completion of the 'Waterloo' album. In retrospect, it seems most likely that the inbuilt British prejudice against artists emerging from the Eurovision contest ruined the record's chances, although one or two other factors may have also contributed. It seems possible that the wrong song was chosen as the A side of the record, that is, the side Epic hoped might be played on the radio; 'I've Been Waiting For You', a well performed medium paced ballad written and produced by Benny and Björn, would have been a more suitable choice. The solo vocal parts are sung by Agnetha, while both girls sing the choruses, in a style which would be repeated some months later in 'S.O.S.'. The song is magnificently produced in a manner which the great Phil Spector, creator of 1960s hits for groups like The Ronettes and The Crystals, would probably have appreciated, and the result is almost a great track. The only reservations concern the lyrics, on which Stig Anderson collaborated with Björn and Benny: at times, especially at the start of the song, they seem awkward, which may have been the reason for its relegation to the B side. 'So Long', by contrast, although perfectly adequate lyrically, is possibly a little too furious in tempo for their 1974 audience. Starting with an instrumental crescendo, which owes far more to hard rock than pop, it seems to fall between two stools. Nevertheless, if either side had been released to an open-minded public, things might have been different, as both sides are instrumentally superb, a particular highlight being the guitar playing on 'I've Been Waiting For You', which is highly reminiscent of George Harrison's playing on his charttopping classic, 'My Sweet Lord'. Perhaps one day these tracks may receive the attention they deserve...

Of course, ABBA had little time to worry about their shortcomings in the British charts; after one week back in Stockholm, they were due back on the road for the second leg of their tour. Originally scheduled to include five dates in Britain during December 1974, the tour was drastically pruned for economic reasons, Polar Music having learned that expenses incurred in taking a twenty strong party and all their equipment around Europe had eroded any profit from the first block of dates. As a result, the group spent Christmas at home in Sweden in comparative peace, although Benny, Björn and Stig no doubt spent much of the holiday period writing and planning the next ABBA LP.

By January 10th, 1975, they were back on the road for the last stage of the tour, which took them through Norway and Sweden before finishing in Stockholm on January 20th. After the rather disappointing crowds at the start of the tour, the Scandinavian section was a complete triumph with capacity audiences everywhere. Northern Europe was obviously under control – but there were pressing problems elsewhere. In the United States, 'Waterloo' had made the Top 10, 'Ring Ring' had failed to dent the charts at all, and 'Honey, Honey' had been a medium sized hit. Progress on the other side of the Atlantic was reasonable... but in Britain, ABBA were back at the starting gate....

1975
NO TOUR – AND NOT MUCH OF A HIT

After finishing their tour, ABBA maintained a low profile for a few months, spending much of their time ensconced in the recording studio working on the eponymously titled 'ABBA' album, which eventually took almost a whole year to complete. Björn and Benny spent the first part of the time writing new songs, sometimes helped by Stig, then began to prepare the arrangements before actually recording the album which they, of course, also produced. Björn told *Record Mirror*: "We're concentrating on making a really first class and polished album." Having made inroads into the US with 'Waterloo', it was essential that a new album should reflect a positive direction, to continue the group's progress and enhance their international status.

One or two other things materialised during the first part of 1975, not least the original appearance of one of the most famous quotes concerning ABBA, and in particular, Agnetha, who, it was claimed, possessed the sexiest bottom in popular music. Probably because many feel that there's a good deal of truth in the assertion, it has been constantly repeated ever since, although at one time, a rival posterior, that of Suzi Quatro, also gathered a certain amount of critical support... Rather more relevant to music was the fact that Björn, Benny and Stig had agreed to write a Eurovision song for their old friends Svenne & Lotta. In 1975, Eurovision was being held in Stockholm, following the normal procedure of the winning nation hosting the next contest, and the song chosen for Svenne & Lotta was one of the tracks they were polishing for the upcoming 'ABBA' album. While 'Bang-A-Boomerang' is certainly a very typical Eurovision Song Contest title, the quality of the song was rather superior to routine Eurovision fodder. Unfortunately, the Polar Music team were unsuccessful with their entry on this occasion, although Svenne & Lotta enjoyed a sizeable Scandinavian hit when they issued the song as a single.

April 4th, 1975
I DO, I DO, I DO, I DO, I DO/ROCK ME (Epic EPC 3229)

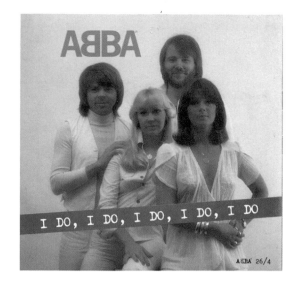

How not to follow a flop... 'I Do' was far from the best song from the forthcoming album – as *Melody Maker* noted, "this single is so bad, it hurts" – but as Björn said in an interview in England, "We decided to release it because it was a very commercial record and stood a better chance of making the charts in Britain." He went on to explain that ABBA felt impelled to pull out of the projected British tour a few months earlier because "there were already something like thirty or forty groups on the road in England at that time, so we decided to leave it for a bit."

In comparison with what had already been heard from ABBA, this single was obviously something of a novelty, with its smooth big band sound redolent of the music popular during the Second World War years nearly a generation earlier. However commercial Björn may have thought it, British record buyers were happy to resist its charms – until, more than three months after its release, the single crept into the chart. A proportion of this belated success was due to the fact that two of the Epic Records promotion team hired top hats, white ties and tails, while a third dressed in a long and very ornate wedding dress, and the trio spent a day being driven around London in a Rolls Royce limousine pretending to stage a marriage at each of the major radio stations. It was nothing more than a typical showbiz publicity stunt, of course, but it did gain a few extra radio plays for the single which finally nudged it into the bottom of the chart, where it remained for six weeks, peaking at No.38 during August. Few would argue that this was one of ABBA's greatest singles; in no way did it reflect the exciting direction in which the group were moving musically. That could be far better detected in the B side, 'Rock Me', which is perhaps the rawest single ABBA ever released. In other countries, 'I Do' was released as the follow-up to 'S.O.S.', which gave it a more substantial foundation than the commmercial failure of 'So Long'.

By the time that 'I Do' had made its brief chart appearance, British journalists had been given the chance to hear several more tracks from the 'ABBA' album, and a certain amount of criticism was levelled at the group for not choosing 'S.O.S.' as the new single in preference to 'I Do'. Björn defended his position by saying "It's very difficult for us to get away from the Eurovision tag, especially in England where people seem to expect us to produce records in the 'Waterloo' vein. I'd have preferred to release 'S.O.S.', because it gives our fans much more of a clue about the musical direction we're heading for – I think people are gradually realising that we aren't just a mediocre pop band."

(Left) On stage in Stockholm, 1975

831 596-2

June 7th, 1975
ABBA (LP) (Epic EPC 80835)
Side One: MAMMA MIA/HEY, HEY, HELEN/TROPICAL LOVELAND/
S.O.S./MAN IN THE MIDDLE/BANG-A-BOOMERANG
Side Two: I DO, I DO, I DO, I DO, I DO/ROCK ME/INTERMEZZO NO.1/
I'VE BEEN WAITING FOR YOU/SO LONG

Remarkably, each of the 11 tracks on 'ABBA' was released in single form either in the UK or US or both, a claim which few other albums could make. Despite this, it must have been one of the slowest albums ever to reach the chart, taking a full six months to make the British Top 50, where it stayed from January to March, 1976. Two smash singles finally forced it into the chart at the start of the New Year, which was when people began to re-assess its worth. Until then few people had been sufficiently interested to investigate the record carefully, and this had been reflected in some of the reviews, *Disc's* Harry Doherty, who later became one of the group's greatest supporters, ended his review with "Stick to singles, ABBA. You're just a mediocre album band." He's probably changed his mind now and wishes he had been less hasty... Another reviewer complained "ABBA's songs are relentlessly trivial" and a third concluded that the album was a thoroughly middle of the road effort. They weren't all so critical, of course: *Melody Maker*, although devoting very little space to the album, ended their review with "interesting album, good strong musicianship, good tunes," while a provincial journalist wrote "a group who bring a startling professionalism and integrity to their work, that's worth anybody's time and money."

Six of the tracks were written by Benny and Björn with assistance from Stig, while the other five were straightforward Andersson/Ulvaeus compositions. Most of the record should be familiar to anyone who has heard ABBA's singles, although several songs might not be immediately recognisable as ABBA recordings, notably the gentle reggae song, 'Tropical Loveland' (which was released in America as the B side of 'Mamma Mia'), 'Man in the Middle', which one critic described as "a disastrous attempt at social awareness," and 'Bang-a-Boomerang', the song written for Svenne & Lotta's abortive Eurovision quest. Perhaps the most interesting track is the instrumental featuring Benny's keyboard pyrotechnics, 'Intermezzo No.1', which was originally given the title 'Mama'. Somewhat reminiscent of the kind of thing 'serious' rock groups like Emerson, Lake and Palmer have attempted in its fusion of classical music and rock instruments, its lasting appeal was demonstrated by the acclaim it was accorded when Benny played it on the 1979 tour. Benny, in fact, seems to be the dominant musician on this album, his clavinet (a keyboard instrument) in particular making its presence felt to great effect. All in all, a fine album, although very few people (myself regrettably included) recognised it as such immediately.

In Sweden, 'ABBA' was a runaway best seller, with advance orders exceeding 150,000, a figure never previously dreamt of in ABBA's native land. By the end of 1975, sales of the album had nearly reached half a million, meaning that five per cent of the country's entire population had purchased a copy. In the UK, the equivalent would be sales of more than three million copies, and in America, around twelve million, a figure which very few albums indeed ever achieve. But perhaps even more significant was the fact that the 'ABBA' album marked the beginning of the group's success behind the Iron Curtain. During June 1975, a leading Polish politician visited Sweden, and Polish newspapers devoted maximum coverage to his visit. One paper featured a photograph of ABBA, also publishing the address of their fan club in Sweden, as a result of which a deluge of letters arrived from Polish pop fans. Eventually, increasing demand led to ABBA's records being released in several communist countries, starting with Poland and East Germany. In both countries, the record industry was state-owned, and only a limited amount of money was available for the purchase of recordings from the West each year, but it wasn't long before Poland used all its available finance for foreign recordings to buy ABBA records. Even so, the popularity of their records was so great that albums by ABBA became very marketable commodities on the illegal black market. Eventually, even the USSR was

allowing ABBA records to be released, although once again they had to be licensed through the state-controlled record company.

On June 24th, 1975, ABBA embarked on a two week tour of the Swedish public parks, the 'Folkpark' circuit. This was obviously to atone for the previous year's cancellation, although this time the group were actually in a far better position to ensure that two weeks away from the action would not detract from their international efforts. Having already prepared their stage act, and rehearsed to concert pitch a few months earlier, it was comparatively simple to achieve the same standard again. However, Stig Anderson, being the astute businessman he undoubtedly is, decreed that ABBA would not perform for less than sixty per cent of the tour's profits, a move which infuriated several local promoters, who suggested that Stig was trying to bankrupt them. They had no need to be worried – by this time, ABBA were so enormously popular in their own country that the two weeks went by almost without a hitch, and everyone, including the promoters, reaped more than adequate financial rewards from the tour. The only problem occurred when two of the dates had to be postponed and re-scheduled for the end of the tour, as Agnetha's troublesome throat infection had made an unwelcome reappearance and it became obvious that something would have to be done to prevent future recurrences. Plans for performances in Britain and America were already being finalised and any cancellations could have unhappy repercussions.

September 19th, 1975
S.O.S./MAN IN THE MIDDLE (Epic EPC 3576)

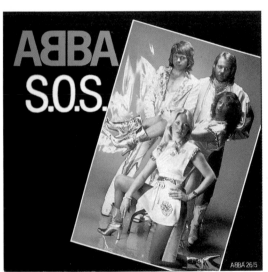

This was the single which ended the long period of uncertainty surrounding ABBA's destiny in Britain. After entering the charts within days of release, it remained in the Top 50 for more than two months, peaking at No.6. In America, it was also a Top 10/Top 20 single, depending on which chart you favoured, and in both countries it was the single which finally established ABBA as long term prospects. In Germany, 'S.O.S.' was voted best pop song of the year, while in the US, it won the BMI award as one of the most played records of the year... and around the world it placed the group squarely on the map, convincing even the most vociferous cynics that here was an act to be reckoned with. Over the rest of the decade and beyond, ABBA were one of the most consistently popular groups in the world.

September 1975 also saw the group making their first lengthy promotional trip to the United States, where they spent a hectic two weeks making television appearances, although not performing any live concerts. Agnetha had been predictably unhappy about the prospect of leaving her daughter at home for such a long period, and it was eventually agreed that Linda should accompany them to the States, although Agnetha subsequently regretted the decision, as Linda, who was not yet three years old, found the extremely long flight a less than pleasant experience.

Back in Sweden, Benny and Björn knuckled down to their other production commitments, in particular to an album for Ted Gardestad. It was around this time that Anni-Frid and Agnetha released solo albums, although neither performed any of the solo material on international tours. Anni-Frid, whose album was titled 'Frida Ensam', was quite interested in briefly resuming her solo career but was talked out of it by Stig, who felt that any appearances might detract from the ABBA group effort, which was now entering its most successful phase. Even so, rumours circulating in Sweden suggested that Anni-Frid was on the point of leaving ABBA, particularly when 'Frida Alone' topped the album chart, selling 100,000 copies. Agnetha's solo effort, 'Eleven Women In One House', was less successful, although for Stig Anderson, it marked the end of the long and exasperating period during which Polar Music had been compelled to pay a percentage of ABBA's profits to CBS-Cupol Records, to whom Agnetha was exclusively contracted until the end of 1975.

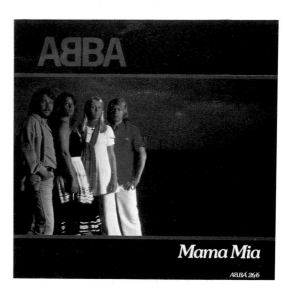

Note the spelling error on the single sleeve below

November 14th, 1975
MAMMA MIA/INTERMEZZO NO.1 (Epic EPC 3790)

Despite one reviewer's suggestion that 'Mamma Mia' was "not as catchy as 'S.O.S.'," this single became ABBA's second British chart-topper, although for some time it looked as though it might not quite be strong enough to displace the massive Christmas hit of 1975, 'Bohemian Rhapsody' by Queen, which had held the Number One spot for an amazing nine weeks. It wasn't until the end of January 1976 that 'Mamma Mia' finally managed to depose it, carrying 'ABBA' into the album chart in its wake. When the group came to Britain for a few days, Björn was obviously aware that they had made the decisive breakthrough, as he told one of the music papers: "This is the first time we've come over to England and met with some kind of response. We never felt we should forget about conquering England, we just thought it was extremely difficult to reach the British people, but we have so much self-confidence that we thought that sooner or later it was bound to happen here; fortunately, we've been proved right." Björn also pointed out that in Sweden, the Eurovision success "was like winning the World Cup," and he mentioned the possibility of a UK tour: "We're waiting until British audiences really want us to play here. Besides, you don't really need to tour if you don't need the money..."

'Mamma Mia' was also the breakthrough single in Australia, where audiences became totally besotted with ABBA. Several singles had been released there previously, but it was an early example of ABBA's world-famous promotional films which provided the necessary impetus, leading to a situation where five ABBA singles soon nestled in the Australian Top 10 simultaneously, while a compilation album, 'Best Of ABBA' (which was not released in either Britain or America) sold the staggering total of more than 850,000 copies in a country with a population of less than 14 million people. Another remarkable statistic indicating the group's incredible popularity...

In America, things were a little different: ABBA records were often released in a different order, and often some months behind the rest of the world. 'S.O.S.' was a big hit at the end of 1975, and was followed by 'I Do, I Do, I Do, I Do, I Do', which reached the Top 20 during May 1976, although the 'ABBA' album had been a comparative failure, not selling strongly enough to make the Top 150. 'Mamma Mia', the final A side to be culled from the 'ABBA' album, was a Top 40 hit, although only just... it was obvious that there was still plenty of work to be done in the New World.

The final month of 1975 saw ABBA taking a much needed rest, although for Björn and Benny, the holiday season was a time to add the finishing touches to a couple of new songs which would be heard by many millions of fans throughout the world during 1976, 'Fernando' and 'Dancing Queen'. For Agnetha, Christmas was far less festive – her throat problems had been diagnosed as tonsilitis, and it was decided that the break afforded her an ideal opportunity to go into hospital to have her tonsils removed, a particularly painful operation if the patient is an adult. It was not a happy time for Agnetha, although she was still able to gain the admiration of the others when, in a bid to ensure that her throat gave her no more problems, she also gave up smoking...

1976
SUCCESS SUSTAINED – BIG TIME IN BRITAIN

Apart from anything else, 1976 turned out to be ABBA's most successful year in Britain up to that time. By the end of January, 'Mamma Mia' had knocked 'Bohemian Rhapsody' off the top of the singles chart, although even this caused a little controversy in the ABBA camp when they came to Britain early in the year to perform their hit on *Top Of The Pops*, the most influential TV pop show in Britain at the time. It was a rule that as many artists as possible should recreate their hit records specially for the programme, and in order to achieve this, a backing track was normally recorded shortly before the show to enable the artist to sing live when it was broadcast. ABBA had previously experienced some problems with the resident *Top Of The Pops* orchestra, who were, after all, in the difficult position of having to provide backings for several different types of music within the duration of the show; to ensure an accurate reproduction of 'Mamma Mia', it was decided that ABBA would bring three of their regular backing musicians to London. Accordingly, they arrived with guitarist Lars (Lasse) Wellander and drummer Ola Brunkert, plus Kaj Hogberg, who was deputizing for their normal bass man, Rutger Gunnarsson. Even with this specialised help, they were unable to duplicate the record to their satisfaction and subsequently rarely appeared live on *Top Of The Pops*. Instead they preferred to supply this and similar shows around the world with the inventive promotional films which became such a feature of their hitmaking career, and which surely contributed strongly to their consistent tenure at the top of the charts. This procedure also had the advantage of dispensing with the need for much of the endless travel which would otherwise have been necessary to promote their record releases.

While ABBA were in Britain, they took the opportunity to meet several journalists, and Benny and Björn made some strong points in their interviews. Their main area of concern was the way in which the British press tended to regard them as a pop-orientated singles group. As Benny said, "The singles aren't really representative of everything we do. I wish we could also be appreciated as a band which sells albums," and one journalist was moved to agree, writing "The image ABBA portray on their singles is totally mis-representative of their creative talent." It was also found that ABBA rarely released singles in their homeland, ostensibly because they didn't receive radio play. An alarming thought – if they don't play ABBA, what kind of music do they play on Swedish radio?

By coincidence, among the other artists featured on *Top Of The Pops* in the same week as ABBA were 10cc, and one member of that group, Graham Gouldman, revealed that he had heard Anni-Frid's Swedish version of the 10cc hit, 'Wall Street Shuffle'. Apparently, his au pair was Swedish, and had been sent a copy of Anni-Frid's record by a friend. The track had been included on the 'Frida Alone' album, as had a song called 'Fernando'...

March 3rd, 1976
FERNANDO/HEY, HEY, HELEN (Epic EPC 4036)

Anni-Frid's solo version of 'Fernando' had only been released in Scandinavia, but had been successful enough for Benny, Björn and Stig to write an English lyric and re-record the song as an official ABBA single. It entered the British chart soon after release, but, ironically enough, was blocked from the Number One position for six weeks by the 1976 Eurovision Song Contest winner, 'Save Your Kisses For Me'. The song was performed by Brotherhood of Man, an English group which, like ABBA, comprised two males and two females, and which many observers felt was modelled completely on ABBA's highly successful blueprint. Eventually, during the second week of May 1976, consistent sales of 'Fernando' exceeded those of the Brotherhood of Man single, and ABBA were back on top, where they remained for four weeks. The B side of the single, 'Hey, Hey Helen', became the ninth of the 11 tracks on the 'ABBA' album to be released in single form, but, of course, it wasn't the B side which was the selling point. 'Fernando' went on to become the biggest ABBA single of their early period, racking up world-wide sales estimated at more than six million copies even before the year was out.

During March, ABBA made a brief promotional tour of Australia, where, need it be said, they were extremely well received. One of the main highlights of the visit was a 45 minute TV special, which was watched by a greater percentage of Australian viewers than had viewed Neil Armstrong's Moon landing in July 1969! A perfect introduction to a new audience who would be seeing the group performing in the flesh less than a year later....

March 26th, 1976
GREATEST HITS (LP) (Epic EPC 69218)
Side One: S.O.S./HE IS YOUR BROTHER/RING RING/HASTA MANANA/
NINA PRETTY BALLERINA/HONEY HONEY/SO LONG
Side Two: I DO, I DO, I DO, I DO, I DO/PEOPLE NEED LOVE/
BANG-A-BOOMERANG/ANOTHER TOWN, ANOTHER TRAIN/MAMMA MIA/
DANCE (WHILE THE MUSIC STILL GOES ON)/ WATERLOO/FERNANDO

This, ABBA's third album to be released in Britain, differed from most 'Greatest Hits' compilations in that no less than five of the tracks were completely new as far as British audiences were concerned. (One of these was 'Fernando', of course – few other artists in 1976 would have dared to include their current single, only released a matter of days before, on a 'Greatest Hits' collection!). Of the tracks already familiar, five came from their debut 'Waterloo' album, and five more from its 'ABBA' follow-up, and these included six single A sides, with 'Fernando' increasing that total to seven.

Equally interesting are the four tracks which remain. Two of them, 'People Need Love' and 'Another Town, Another Train', had been released in America during 1972/3, although they had been attributed to 'Björn & Benny with Svenska Flicka'. As previously mentioned, 'People Need Love', their first single for Playboy Records, had been close to the Top 100 when distribution problems prevented it from rising further, although there were indications of a possible hit. Björn and Benny's other Playboy single was 'Rock'n Roll Band' (released in Britain as the B side of 'Ring Ring'), backed with 'Another Town, Another Train', while in Sweden, the follow up to 'People Need Love' had been 'He Is Your Brother'. The fourth new track, 'Nina Pretty Ballerina', dates from the same period. The inclusion of these four tracks was particularly valuable to anyone interested in ABBA's pre-fame history, although they are also interesting in their own right, displaying all the skill and innovation characterising their later recordings. 'He Is Your Brother', for example, bears a noticeable resemblance to The Mamas & Papas, the pioneering American group from the 1960s to whom ABBA said they would like to be compared, while 'Nina Pretty Ballerina' is inventively produced with sound effects of trains and audience applause to illustrate the song's story. 'People Need Love' has a sound very similar to the British group, Blue Mink, who had a big hit in 1969 with 'Melting Pot', although since this is one source of possible inspiration to

which ABBA never admitted, the similarity may be purely coincidental. Another more likely influence on their earlier work is the Australian group, The Seekers, who enjoyed worldwide popularity at the time Björn was a member of The Hootenanny Singers: certainly, 'Another Town, Another Train' could easily be mistaken for a Seekers record! As examples of ABBA's progress, these tracks are essential: by the time 'Greatest Hits' was released, ABBA's own sound had become unique and distinctive, whereas previously their influences were readily apparent as they sought their own style.

In Britain, the album was one of the first to be advertised on television and was helped to a flying start by advance orders running into six figures, which ensured a speedy chart entry – four weeks later, it was at Number One, where it remained for nine weeks. After a 14 week gap, it actually managed to regain the top position for two more weeks in October 1976, and altogether featured in the British album chart for more than two and a half years, amassing sales totalling nearly three million copies!

In America, where it wasn't released until the end of 1976, the album appears to have been a slow but steady seller – while its highest chart position was only just inside the Top 50 (extremely strange, as 'Fernando' was streaking into the US Top 20 at the time), the group were eventually presented with a platinum disc for sales of more than one million copies. *Cashbox* magazine obviously felt it was going to be a smash hit, when their reviewer wrote "ABBA is the perfect example of what European pop music is all about – the vocals are clean and instantly dominant, the melodies catchy and generously spiced with good pop hooks. Retailers take notice – this is one record that's going to sell very well in the racks." Another US music industry trade magazine, *Record World*, was a little less enthusiastic and perhaps more accurate when their critic noted "The group's identity lacks the definition that would make it a household name." The fact that many Americans still seem to have ignored 'Greatest Hits' is one of the most puzzling chapters in the group's history, but despite American reservations, world sales of the album had already exceeded five million copies by the end of 1976.

April 1976 saw fresh accolades poured on the group from all sides, especially from Turkey, where ABBA were proclaimed 'top group of 1976', and Australia, where their TV special had stimulated a fan worship similar to America's discovery of the Beatles 12 years earlier. 'Fernando' stood at Number One in the Australian singles chart, 'Ring Ring' was at No.4, 'Rock Me' at 5, 'Mamma Mia' at 20 and 'S.O.S.' at 22, while all three ABBA albums nestled in the Top 20. This eruption, however, was no help to one unfortunate Australian, the liaison officer for the Red Cross Blood Bank in the City of Sydney, whose name happened to be David Abba. After several hundred people had phoned to sing him the first few bars of 'Fernando', Mr. Abba got his story in the local newspapers, but also took his phone off the hook until a new ex-directory number could be arranged! Perhaps the most alarming aspect of the entire affair was that Mr.Abba claimed never to have heard of the famous group until he was besieged by all his humorous callers!

During the first half of the year, much of ABBA's time had been spent in the recording studio preparing material for the next album, which was due for release before the end of the year, but on June 18th, 1976, the group took a day off for a special reason. They were to perform a tribute to Silvia Sommerlath, a very important Swedish lady indeed, at a gala held on the day before her marriage to Sweden's King, Carl Gustaf. Sweden's future Queen was entertained by all kinds of famous national artists, but the only pop act invited to participate was ABBA, who performed the most appropriate 'Dancing Queen', which would become their next single. Strangely, even this royal recognition caused ABBA problems, when several Swedish newspapers erroneously assumed that 'Dancing Queen' had been specially written for the occasion by Benny, Stig and Björn. This was patently untrue, as the song had been mentioned six months before as one of the tracks completed over the 1975 Christmas holiday, but it seems that all too often, the Swedish media were eager to criticise the most successful entertainers their country had ever produced...

During July, ABBA were back in Britain, although probably for no other reason than to inspect possible venues for a projected concert debut due to take place at the start of 1977. Björn in particular remembered the Earls Court Arena, because that was where he had seen The Rolling Stones perform, but ultimately the capital's prime concert auditorium, the Royal Albert

Hall, was selected for their London dates. It was also during this month that ABBA's official British fan club was set in motion; within six months, over 5,000 British ABBA fanatics had joined. This, however, was a mere trifle compared to the membership the club would be able to boast in 1977.

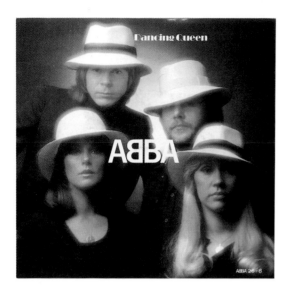

August 6th, 1976
DANCING QUEEN/THAT'S ME (Epic EPC 4499)

This, ABBA's third British chart-topper in a row, paired two tracks from the 'Arrival' album, which was released later in the year. 'Dancing Queen' entered the charts soon after release, and in two weeks was at Number One, where it repelled all-comers for six of its 15 week chart stay. The A side was one of ABBA's most instantly identifiable recordings, a factor which tended to deflect the spotlight from the Latin-American flavoured 'That's Me', a fine recording in its own right. One of the group's biggest selling UK singles, 'Dancing Queen' reached the half million mark during its first month of release, and eventually clocked up sales of more than 850,000 in Britain alone, also topping the chart in Holland, Australia, West Germany, Belgium, Norway, Sweden, Denmark, Switzerland and Austria. More importantly, it became the first ABBA single to top the American charts, when it was finally released there in the early part of 1977.

Coinciding with the release of 'Dancing Queen', it was officially announced that ABBA would be embarking on a major tour at the start of 1977 and would be performing live in London for the first time. In order to present a concert sound comparable to that achieved on their records, the group was to be augmented by a touring party of no less than 16 singers and musicians – five keyboard players, three guitarists and four backing singers, plus a saxophone player and a rhythm section of bass, drums and percussion. The group also gave journalists their impression of how their audience was made up. Apparently, they felt that the major part of their following was divided between those aged from seven to 14, and those over 20, while the older teenagers between the two ranges seemed to be much less heavily represented. Worldwide sales figures for ABBA's records were also published: of the singles, 'Fernando' led the field with sales of over six million, followed by 'Waterloo' with five million, 'S.O.S.' with four million, 'Mamma Mia' with three and a half million, and 'Dancing Queen' with three million, while 'Honey Honey', 'I Do' and 'So Long' had all passed the one million mark. In terms of albums, 'Greatest Hits' was out in front with five million sales, followed by 'ABBA' with four million and 'Waterloo' with three million. It was also revealed that these figures could have been substantially higher – police had confiscated a cache of 700,000 pirated ABBA albums, inferior imitations of the genuine article with poor sound quality and black and white sleeves replacing the real thing, although usually featuring the same picture. These were discovered in Australia, but in those days before the advent of CD, it was also estimated that for every genuine ABBA LP sold in Hong Kong, as many as five pirated copies were being purchased by unsuspecting record buyers. This was just one of many methods being used to exploit the group, and during 1976, efforts were made to prevent pirates in Britain from producing unauthorised merchandise which featured either ABBA's name or their photograph.

Meanwhile, ABBA records were reaching places where pop records had rarely been heard. Stig Anderson had negotiated a deal with the authorities in the USSR to supply them with copies of the 'Greatest Hits' album, and insisted on being paid in American dollars, as Russian currency was virtually worthless in the Western world. When asked about the extent of ABBA's global success, Stig replied "We sell everywhere, except in China, North Korea and Vietnam." Another Eastern European country, Poland, invited ABBA to Warsaw to make a TV special shortly before the release of the 'Arrival' album, and their acceptance contributed strongly to the album selling over three quarters of a million copies in Poland. Sweden also finally decided that a TV spectacular should be made about their incredibly successful export, and during the Autumn of 1976, prepared the hour long *ABBA From The Beginning*, also apparently known as *ABBA-Dabba-Doo*. At the end of October, ABBA were back in America, where 'Fernando' was high in the charts. Their schedule included eight nationally networked TV shows in Canada and the

DANCING QUEEN MAKES IT A HAT TRICK

USA, and this afforded practically every North American inhabitant an introduction to ABBA. One of the TV appearances was on the *Dinah Shore Show*, hosted by the famous singer of the 1940s, who told Anni-Frid and Benny that she was surprised at how long they had been engaged without actually getting married. She offered them the opportunity to marry in front of the television cameras, where they'd be watched by several million people, but the invitation was politely declined, the couple indicating that they would prefer to postpone their wedding until they felt they were ready... Another highlight of the trip occurred when the group were presented with an award from the British newspaper, *The Sun*, as the most popular entertainers to appear on British television during 1976. The award was presented by Anthony Newley, ex-husband of film star Joan Collins and himself a British chart topper at the start of the 1960s with 'Why' and 'Do You Mind'.

November 5th, 1976
ARRIVAL (LP) (Epic EPC 86018)
Side One: WHEN I KISSED THE TEACHER/DANCING QUEEN/MY LOVE, MY LIFE/DUM DUM DIDDLE/KNOWING ME, KNOWING YOU
Side Two: MONEY, MONEY, MONEY/THAT'S ME/WHY DID IT HAVE TO BE ME/ TIGER/ARRIVAL

After ABBA's enormous successes earlier in the year, this was an album which a great many people were eagerly anticipating. In Britain, advance orders amounted to 300,000 copies – and just how impressive this figure was can be judged from the fact that the previous biggest advance order had been for 225,000 copies of 'Horizon', the album by The Carpenters. Worldwide advance orders for 'Arrival' were worth more than £5,000,000 and the album was simultaneously released in 34 different countries!

In Britain, 'Arrival' entered the album chart at No.6 one week after release, but was prevented from reaching the top for several weeks, first by Glen Campbell's '20 Golden Greats', and over the Christmas period by Queen's 'A Day At The Races'. However, it finally reached Number One in the first week of 1977, after which it dropped back, only to return to the top for a triumphant nine week spell in April/May 1977. 'Arrival' also achieved the distinction of being the first ABBA album to be certified gold in the US.

Reviewers were much more enthusiastic about 'Arrival' than they had been about either 'ABBA' or 'Waterloo'. 'Dancing Queen' and 'That's Me' were familiar, of course, but of the other eight tracks, the one selected for most praise was 'Tiger', which was freely tipped as a suitable follow up to 'Dancing Queen'. 'Why Did It Have To Be Me', on which Björn sang lead, also attracted attention for its rhythm & blues styled backing but, strangely enough, few critics commented on the tracks which would become ABBA's next two singles, 'Money, Money, Money' and 'Knowing Me, Knowing You'. The former, however, was correctly identified as being rooted in a German cabaret style and one critic noted that the lyric seemed to have been inspired by 10cc's 'Wall Street Shuffle', which, of course, Anni-Frid had recently recorded on her solo album. Ironically, 'Money, Money, Money' was one of only two tracks on which Frida was the featured lead singer, the other being 'Knowing Me, Knowing You'. Agnetha meanwhile, took the lead on 'When I Kissed The Teacher' and 'My Love, My Life', the latter also being covered by British singer Jonathan King, whose version featured his impersonation of Roxy Music leader Bryan Ferry.

Record Mirror called 'Arrival' "ABBA's best yet," and another critic was of the opinion that it had "elevated their music to new heights of commercial refinement." *New Musical Express* was less enthusiastic, calling 'Money, Money, Money' "patent rubbish," while a similar position was taken by another paper, whose critic felt that 'Dum Dum Diddle' possessed "the corniest lyrics of all time." But perhaps the most intriguing track on 'Arrival' was the title song, basically an instrumental, which, as several reviewers noted, sounded almost Scottish and rather similar to a British hit of 1971, 'I Will Return', performed by Phil Cordell under the name of Springwater. 'Arrival' itself could easily have been a hit single, but then three other tracks from the album were to achieve that feat...

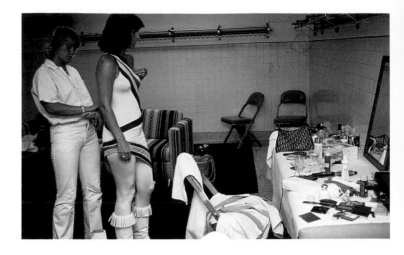

(Below) The futuristic cartoon sleeve used on the 'Greatest Hits' LP, never released in the UK

Side 1)
1. *** SOS   3.22
2. * HE IS YOUR BROTHER   3.15
      (B. Andersson, B. Ulvaeus)
3. * RING RING   3.00
      (B. Andersson, S. Anderson,
      B. Ulvaeus, N. Sedaka, P. Cody)
4. ** HASTA MANANA   3.05
5. * NINA PRETTY BALLERINA   2.50
      (B. Andersson, B. Ulvaeus)
6. ** HONEY HONEY   2.55
7. *** SO LONG   3.06
      (B. Andersson, B. Ulvaeus)

Side 2)
1. *** I DO, I DO, I DO, I DO, I DO   3.15
2. * PEOPLE NEED LOVE   2.42
      (B. Andersson, B. Ulvaeus)
3. *** BANG-A-BOOMERANG   2.50
4. * ANOTHER TOWN,
      ANOTHER TRAIN   3.10
      (B. Andersson, B. Ulvaeus)
5. *** MAMMA MIA   3.32
6. ** DANCE (WHILE THE MUSIC
      STILL GOES ON)   3.05
      (B. Andersson, B. Ulvaeus)
7. ** WATERLOO   2.46

All songs not otherwise noted are written by
B. Andersson, S. Anderson, B. Ulvaeus
All songs published by Union Songs AB
Produced by Benny Andersson & Björn Ulvaeus
Recorded at Metronome Studio & Glen Studio
Engineer: Michael B. Tretow
Painting front cover by Hans Arnold
Photo by Bengt H. Malmqvist
Album Design by Rune Söderqvist
Agnetha by courtesy of CBS Records AB

℗ 1972-73-74-75 Polar Music AB

1976 All rights assigned to
Polar Music International AB

* From LP "Ring Ring" POLS 242, 1973
** From LP "Waterloo" POLS 252, 1974
*** From LP "ABBA" POLS 262, 1975

POLS 266

GREATESTHITS

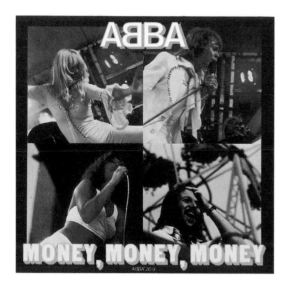

November 11th, 1976
MONEY, MONEY, MONEY/CRAZY WORLD
(Epic EPC 4713)

Released one week after the 'Arrival' album, this single was a predictable success, although it was the only ABBA single between the end of 1975 and the spring of 1978 to fail to reach the top of the British chart, being thwarted in this instance by the unlikely trio of Chicago, Showaddywaddy and Johnny Mathis. Even so, it hung in the chart until well into 1977 in the course of a 12 week residency. The B side, 'Crazy World', was something of a rarity, as it was not included on any ABBA album at the time. Sung by Björn, it's a straightforward ballad detailing the none too original story of boyfriend who sees a strange male entering his girlfriend's house, and is desperately depressed until he discovers that the stranger is in fact the girlfriend's brother. For once, it actually sounds like a B side, and, judging by the simplicity of the production, may have been recorded some considerable time before its release. In America, 'Money, Money, Money' was issued a year later, and even then was relatively unsuccessful, hovering just outside the Top 50.

On November 15th, ABBA were due in Britain for a four day promotional visit to coincide with the release of 'Arrival'. In keeping with the sleeve design, it was decided that after ABBA had touched down at London's Heathrow Airport, they would board a helicopter which would take them to a boat on the River Thames, where a crowd of writers, broadcasters and photographers would be waiting. Unfortunately, the chosen day saw London enveloped in dense fog, which resulted in the schedule being seriously disrupted: ABBA had been due to join the boat at 11am, but by the time they actually arrived, it was considerably later, and many of the invited throng had become extremely unhappy. Of course, they really couldn't blame ABBA for the delay...

The end of the year was rather more successful. 'Best Of ABBA' became the biggest-selling cassette of all time in Holland, the group were voted winners of the Carl Allen Award as the most successful songwriters of 1976 in Britain, and the American magazine, *Cashbox,* declared the group Top LP and singles artists of the year. *The Sun,* the English daily newspaper which had previously awarded ABBA a prize as "Top TV Entertainers of the Year," now made them "Top Artists of the Year," and three of their singles were voted among the Top 10 records of 1976 by the newspaper's readers. Things were also beginning to happen in Japan, and in Sweden, record dealers were saying that 'ABBA fever' had become even greater than 'Beatlemania'.

Perhaps the most astonishing statistic occurred when the Royal Albert Hall box office opened to sell tickets for ABBA's 1977 concerts. More than three and a half million ticket applications were received for a total of just over 11,000 seats!

Meanwhile, the group spent the end of 1976 at home, preparing for the upcoming tour, although a totally unfounded news story must certainly have disturbed their concentration. According to reports, they had been involved in a plane crash at West Berlin's Templehof Airport; three members of the group were said to have been killed, the only survivor being Anni-Frid, who was so badly injured that she would never be able to sing again. This was, of course, a malicious fabrication, and the group immediately took great pains to communicate the truth to their representatives in record companies around the world. Closer inspection of the story might have scotched the rumour before it had begun to circulate – Björn and Agnetha always tried to travel on different aircraft, even when heading for the same destination, to preclude any possibility of an accident leaving their daughter Linda an orphan...

Whatever rumours were spread about ABBA, even their detractors would have had to admit that 1976 was a great year for the group. When asked what constituted ABBA's special magic, Benny had replied "Our secret, if there is a secret, is to be completely ruthless about the material we write. If Stig, Björn or I don't like any aspect of one of our songs, we scrap it immediately." Stig, in response to a similar question, cited four rules which he always applied to anything in which he was involved: "Always work very hard. Do your best. Don't forget anything. And don't take life too seriously."

1977
AWARDS
A GOGO

The presentation of numerous awards made for a successful start to 1977: *New Musical Express* declared the group to have been the biggest record sellers of 1976, *Hitmakers* decided that 'Arrival' was the best album of the year (although in chart terms, 'Greatest Hits' was undoubtedly the best-seller), and *Record Mirror* readers voted ABBA Top Group in their annual poll. Elsewhere in Europe, accolades continued to shower them: in Holland, 'Dancing Queen' was the top single of 1976, and in Portugal, Björn and Benny were voted Top Producers and Top Songwriters, with 'Fernando' taking the prize as the year's best recording.

Although this recognition of their talent and success was very gratifying, the group had little opportunity to relax and rest on their laurels, as nearly all their time was taken up preparing and rehearsing for their forthcoming world tour. Thomas Johansson, ABBA's booking agent, had been concentrating on the project since early 1976, talking to promoters in various countries and examining the suitability of venues in Britain and Australia, where the group would be performing for the first time, after concerts around Scandinavia and other parts of Europe. Such detailed preparation was essential as ABBA wanted to leave no stone unturned in their determination to present the best possible stage show to their followers around the world. The costs of travelling, housing the touring party and mounting the show were bound to erode any profit, but making money was not their ultimate motive: the primary purpose of the tour was to give some of their fans the opportunity of seeing them live on stage. Any financial losses could be recouped from record sales generated by the shows.

Eventually, 12 musicians and singers were selected to support ABBA on tour: Lena Andersson, Lena-Maria Gardenas-Lawton and Maritza Horn (backing vocals), Ulf Andersson and Lars Karlsson (saxophones, flutes, etc.) Anders Eljas and Wojciech Ernest (keyboards), Finn Sjoberg and Lasse Wellander (guitars), Rutger Gunnarsson (bass), Ola Brunkert (drums) and Malando Gassama (percussion). Apart from their individual equipment, they were to be amplified through a 20,000 watt stereo P.A. system and illuminated by around 30 tons of lighting! Altogether some 40 people were required to erect, dismantle and manhandle this equipment, all of which called for highly detailed planning and special road and air cargo transport arrangements. The members of the group and management team travelled on scheduled flights, and the cost of the entire operation worked out at around £9,000 for each day the show was on the road.

The end of 1976 and early part of 1977 were spent ironing out every detail, and it was also during this period that Stig revealed to a journalist that ABBA's phenomenal success

was responsible for at least one serious offer per week from companies wishing to buy Polar Music and its most valuable asset, ABBA. This was also the time when Agnetha and Björn began thinking about having another child. Of course, unlike ordinary couples who could simply make the decision and then get on with it, Mr. and Mrs. Ulvaeus had to consider several other people, whose careers would be adversely affected if a new baby were to arrive at an inopportune time, so they consulted with their partners before deciding that the most suitable moment for a new baby to arrive would be close to Christmas, 1977. The tour would be finishing around Easter, leaving Agnetha time to rest before her confinement, as much of the second half of the year would be taken up with recording a new album, whose release would thus coincide with the arrival of the baby. Such careful preparations might appear rather perverse, but as Björn said later, "We didn't want the baby to interfere with the group's progress."

The first leg of the tour, taking in those European countries ABBA had played before, was a great success, and was given an extra boost when the group learned that they had been awarded their first American gold disc, for selling more than one million dollars worth of the 'Arrival' album. During the year, they would add to their American haul when both the 'Greatest Hits' album and the 'Dancing Queen' single would also achieve gold status.

One particular highlight of the tour occurred on the opening date in Oslo, where the group performed before an enthusiastic crowd which included their Royal Highnesses Crown Prince Harald and Crown Princess Sonja of Norway.

February 4th, 1977
KNOWING ME, KNOWING YOU/HAPPY HAWAII
(Epic EPC 4955)

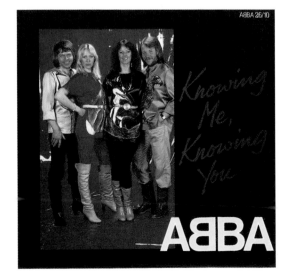

After the comparative failure of 'Money, Money, Money' (if reaching No.3 in the chart could ever be called a failure!), ABBA wasted no time in returning to the pole position in the British singles chart with this, the first of another three consecutive chart-toppers. It was the third single to be extracted from the 'Arrival' album, and although it took a couple of weeks to gather momentum, it reached Number One by the start of April, displacing Manhattan Transfer's 'Chanson D'Amour', and remaining at the top for five of its 13 weeks in the chart.

Sounds magazine declared it pop single for the week, although they called the B side "a very average version of 'Why Did It Have To Be Me'," a description which contains an element of truth. 'Happy Hawaii' is exactly the same musically as their familiar 'Why Did It Have To Be Me', although the lyrics are totally different, and, instead of being sung by Björn, it is sung by the girls, who endow the song with an entirely new flavour. 'Happy Hawaii' had originally been prepared for inclusion on the 'Arrival' album, but was rejected at the last minute, and the raunchier 'Why Did It Have To Be Me' version substituted, after the Hawaiian guitar effects had been removed. Although it was not included on any album at the time, 'Happy Hawaii' was the first in a series of Australian cartoon films which sought to animate ABBA's songs, and its release on record in this form was apparently only at the instigation of business associates who had heard the song and wondered why it remained unreleased. In America at this time, ABBA's current single was 'Dancing Queen', which reached Number One: 'Knowing Me, Knowing You' was issued as a follow up in July, and climbed into the lower half of the Top 20.

A few days into February, ABBA arrived for their first ever live dates in Britain, where they had dominated the charts during the previous year. Five shows were scheduled, one more than planned in the original itinerary of Birmingham, Manchester, Glasgow and London. Demand for tickets at London's Royal Albert Hall had been so great that the group were persuaded to play two performances there on February 14th, but even so, ticket touts were able to do a roaring trade, selling £7.50 seats for £50 or more to desperate fans anxious to see their favourite group.

Once the lights had gone down, the audience was hushed by the sound of a helicopter landing (recalling the sleeve of the 'Arrival' album), whereupon spotlights picked out the four members of ABBA, who erupted into 100 minutes of solid music, packed with just about everything that anyone could have hoped to hear. They played nearly all the tracks from 'Arrival', together with several songs from the first two albums, and a certain amount of new material, the most impressive part of which was the completed section of their projected stage musical, 'The Girl With The Golden Hair'. This provided an element of theatre, as the scenes were linked together by an English actor dressed rather like a character from Dracula, whilst Agnetha and Anni-Frid were dressed identically in blonde wigs, making it difficult to tell them apart, and the 'mini-musical', as the group called it, provided a fitting climax to an excellent show.

While some British critics were predictably ecstatic about the performances, others were, equally predictably, unmoved. *Melody Maker* editor Ray Coleman wrote of "a cold and clinical disappointment" and Tony Parsons from *New Musical Express* called the show "crass, glib and contrived," but *Evening News* critic John Blake called ABBA "the greatest thing since The Beatles," and added "with Anna and Frida looking as they do, I, for one, would be happy even if they didn't sing a note." Even at this late date, some media representatives still called Agnetha 'Anna'...

Most critics, though harbouring some reservations, at least tried to convey what they saw as the group's strong points. *Daily Mail* writer Bart Mills wrote "Their singles have storylines and points of view which are as true an expression of today's well-fed Europe as Chuck Berry's songs were of 1950s America," while Richard Williams, writing in *The Times*, noted that "Their arrangements are their real secret; no-one in the field can match their outstandingly imaginative deployment of pianos, synthesizers and tuned percussion, derived from the innovations of Brian Wilson and Phil Spector." But whatever the critics thought, the fans went home enraptured; the first Swedish performers to appear at the Royal Albert Hall for more than 100 years had good reason to feel pleased with their performance.

It was at this point that the possibility of a film featuring ABBA was first mentioned. It had already been decided that if everything went to plan, the group would not tour during 1978 (Björn and Agnetha's new baby would require a lot of attention, for one thing) and a film would go a long way towards compensating for the lack of live appearances. The original plan was for a documentary, and preliminary shooting was done in Britain, but it was later decided that the film should detail the 1977 tour and also include parts of the mini-musical. (Anni-Frid had already made it clear that if and when the musical was completed, it was not ABBA's intention to appear in a stage version, although it was

conceivable that, at some later date, they might appear in a film adaptation). 'The Girl With The Golden Hair' was built round a fairly simple plot, about a girl from the country who moves to the city in search of stardom, only to become lonely and miserable when she finally achieves her ambition, finding that her only solace is in music...

It was only when ABBA arrived in Australia for the final and most fanatical leg of the tour that the decision was made to alter the concept of the film from a documentary to a light comedy. Swedish film maker Lasse Hallstrom, who had directed their highly acclaimed promotional films, was invited to shape the project and a considerable amount of *ABBA – The Movie* (as it was to be known) was shot in Australia during the first half of March 1977.

The tour wasn't allowed to proceed without some controversy, however: an Australian underground magazine suggested that the four people claiming to be ABBA were actually actors being paid to mime to their records – an interesting but entirely unfounded assumption. Various other problems threatened the smooth running of the operation: the group had to make their Australian debut during a torrential rainstorm, which left their audience of 20,000 soaked to the skin. Conditions were awkward, but ABBA felt they had to perform even though the stage was covered in water, and they received a tremendous reception for their pains. The only casualty was Anni-Frid, who slipped in a puddle during a dance routine and fell rather inelegantly on her backside – fortunately she was only bruised. The next disruption was in Western Australia, where the show was held up until a bomb scare was found to be a hoax.

At another venue, manager Stig Anderson insisted that the ticket allocation be reduced from 40,000 to 20,000, pledging that the group would perform two shows instead of the scheduled one, thus preventing over-crowding and lessening the possibility of injury. In 1973, a young girl had been killed in the melée surrounding the stage at a David Cassidy concert in London (also held in a stadium) and although the promoter was exonerated from any blame, Stig wanted to ensure that no similar danger existed at one of his concerts.

During the first half of 1977, ABBA began to make headlines in other fields. Financial editors of several newspapers began to enquire about their remarkable success, questioning their adamant refusal to become tax exiles like so many of their peers in the entertainment world. After all, Swedish tax laws required them to part with an incredible eighty-five per cent of their income – allowing them to keep slightly more than one eighth of their considerable earnings! Stig explained that the group preferred to stay in Sweden rather than move elsewhere, and indicated that shrewd investment allowed them to enjoy various tax economies. At this point, they owned an art gallery plus property in various Swedish cities, and the conversion of a Stockholm cinema into Polar Music's new recording studio was nearing completion. One example of their shrewd business acumen was the request that payment for their recent Manchester concert be made in either Deutschmarks or Swiss Francs, currencies which held their value better on the European market. Even so, the world tour was said to have cost ABBA £400,000, as opposed to the enormous profit some critics assumed it would make.

Stig Anderson was somewhat upset that, despite their huge financial contribution to the economy of their own country, they had been rewarded by scant recognition. He told *Variety* magazine: "The only reaction we've had from Sweden has been a letter from the Ambassador for Australia. In England, we would have been honoured by the Queen long ago." However, it was obvious that ABBA were great favourites with the general populace of Sweden, as evinced by the 200,000 strong membership of the Swedish branch of their fan club. In Britain too, the ABBA fan club had grown to the point where bigger premises were required to service the needs of its 40,000 members adequately.

MOMENTUM MAINTAINED

In 1977 ABBA released fewer records, in Britain at least, than in any year since their breakthrough. Obviously, much of the time was spent touring and completing their film, but the relative lull in activities set newspaper reporters digging deeper to uncover fresh stories about what was at that time the most popular group in the world. Some of the articles were little more than retreads of the group's history, but others made fascinating reading, especially for those interested in ABBA's money making ability. For example, in July 1977 it was revealed how Stig Anderson had negotiated the sale of ABBA records in several communist-controlled Eastern European countries. Polar Music had joined forces with a Swedish investment company to form a partnership known as Sannes Trading, a business which would export records to Eastern Europe in exchange for oil, vegetables and other goods which could be sold in the West. As no money changed hands, this trade qualified as barter (which did not attract taxation), and was said to be worth the equivalent of £7,000,000 per year, according to the report in a British daily newspaper. In fact, Stig had concluded a multitude of international deals which saw ABBA records released on different labels in different territories: Epic in Britain, Atlantic in the United States, RCA in Australia, Polydor in Germany, and so on. "I don't deal from a money point of view" said Stig, "I see what a company does for us, and whether they do it the right way. I don't believe in world-wide deals – a company can be strong in one region and weak in another. It depends on the people: I go with people I like, and hand pick them territory by territory. A company is no better than its management."

By August, Polar Music was being described as "the most profitable corporation in Sweden," with an income of more than $12 million and an estimated profit for 1977 in the region of £4,000,000.

October 14th, 1977
THE NAME OF THE GAME/I WONDER (DEPARTURE)
(Epic EPC 5750)

These were the first two tracks to appear from 'ABBA – The Album', which would be released at the start of 1978, although this version of 'I Wonder' was actually recorded live in Sydney, Australia, during the tour eight months earlier. The single was an immediate success, entering the British chart within a week of release, and two weeks later reaching Number One, where it remained throughout the month of November. Only after three months did the record drop from the best sellers list.

Melody Maker was somewhat grudging in its praise: "Not a classic, but it'll more than do," while *Sounds* was more effusive: "a satisfying emotive chord sequence and the usual superb vocal harmonies and overall production." What both reviews seemed to ignore was that 'The Name Of The Game' was rather longer than ABBA's previous singles, clocking in at just under five minutes. Because of radio programming strictures, the release of such a long single was somewhat risky, but by this time, ABBA could do no wrong, and the record was a resounding success all over the world, including America, where, although it wasn't released until the early part of 1978, it became a Top 20 smash. Both Anni-Frid and Agnetha sang separate solo parts in 'The Name Of The Game', while the lead vocal in 'I Wonder', which formed part of their 'mini-musical', was sung by Anni-Frid.

By the end of October, the two major items on ABBA's schedule were nearing fruition: their film was almost complete, and Agnetha's pregnancy was drawing to a satisfactory conclusion. The world's press continued to search for ABBA-related stories, many of which concentrated on Polar Music's Stockholm offices, whose walls were decorated with original paintings by the likes of Picasso, Miro and Chagall, among several others, and well over 100 gold and platinum discs, reflecting ABBA's fantastic global success. *Record Mirror* satisfied their readers' demands for new ABBA features by conducting a mock trial, in which reporter Tim Lott accused the group of making bland and sickly music, of insulting their audience with an embarrassing stage act, and of having become a mechanical hit machine. Björn, in an earlier interview with Lott, had responded to the charges levelled against him. He admitted that the tour had not been the triumph they had envisaged: "I think if we did it again, we'd concentrate more on the music than the cabaret, make it not so much a show as a musical concert." To an accusation that the tour was undertaken only to make money, Björn replied "We didn't make any money at all from that tour. In fact,

we lost despite every concert being sold out. We didn't enjoy it much anyway. It was boring – all that time confined to hotel rooms. It's healthy to stand on stage and perform, but I just can't understand how some groups tour for eight, nine, even ten months – it would kill me."

But perhaps the most important news of all concerned Anni-Frid. Newspapers and magazines around the world had discovered and printed the details of her childhood; the story of the German soldier who had apparently deserted her mother, and who was thought to have died when the ship returning him to Germany was sunk. The story appeared in the German magazine *Bravo*, and was read by Andrea Buchinger, an ABBA fan, who recognised the name of Alfred Haase: she had an uncle by that name, and she knew that he had spent part of the war in Norway. Immediately, she contacted her cousin Peter and explained her discovery, whereupon Peter asked his father whether he had known anyone called Synni Lyngstad. It soon became clear that Alfred Haase was in fact Anni-Frid's father, and that the sinking ship story had been fiction.

FRIDA FINDS HER FATHER

Apparently, he had written to Anni-Frid's mother after the war, but had been unaware that she was expecting a baby; more to the point, he was unaware that Synni had died and that Anni-Frid had been brought up in Sweden by her grandmother. The letters had never arrived, due to the post-war confusion and Haase, who was married even before he served in Norway, had settled down with his wife and children, working as office manager of a business in Karlsruhe, West Germany. As soon as he discovered that he was Anni-Frid's father, he telephoned her at Polar Music, and, before long, a tearful meeting united the father and daughter who had been unaware of each other's existence. Initially, they found it difficult to communicate, as Alfred spoke no Swedish, and Anni-Frid little German, but this did little to impair the joy they felt... Anni-Frid had found her father after many years of uncertainty.

It had originally been decided to release ABBA's long awaited album during the final weeks of 1977, and all the recording had been satisfactorily completed by that time. However, a spanner was thrown into the well-oiled works when it was discovered that advance orders were so substantial that it would be impossible to press enough copies to meet the enormous demand. Accordingly, the release was delayed in many countries, including Britain, until 1978 – but this did not detract from the excitement surrounding the film, which was finally ready for unveiling, and at the end of November, ABBA's licensees around the world gathered in Stockholm for a special preview.

BIGGER THAN THE BEATLES

Agnetha, of course, was preoccupied with something rather more important than film shows – and on December 4th, 1977, her second child, Peter Christian Ulvaeus, was born in a Stockholm hospital. Four days later, he appeared before clamouring press photographers and, in the article accompanying their picture, the *Daily Express* took the opportunity to inform the world that ABBA had now overtaken The Beatles in record sales around the world, and had topped the charts in no less than 32 different countries...

The remaining weeks of 1977 saw *ABBA – The Movie* being premièred in Australia, Holland and Scandinavia, while the new album was also released, though only in Sweden (where advance orders had exceeded 600,000 copies) and the other Scandinavian countries. The rest of the world had to wait until 1978. Meanwhile, ABBA's British music publishers, Bocu Music, had been approached by a successful London rowing club, City Orient R.C., who had asked whether ABBA would be prepared to sponsor them. The group, all of whom liked to spend much of their spare time on the water, were happy to give their support and, at the end of 1977, the club were presented with a new boat. Naturally enough, it was named ABBA...

1978
ABBA – THE PLATINUM ALBUM

January 13th, 1978
THE ALBUM (LP) (Epic EPC 86052)
Side One: EAGLE/TAKE A CHANCE ON ME/ONE MAN,ONE WOMAN/
THE NAME OF THE GAME
Side Two: MOVE ON/HOLE IN YOUR SOUL/THE GIRL WITH THE GOLDEN
HAIR – THREE SCENES FROM A MINI-MUSICAL: a) THANK YOU FOR
THE MUSIC b) I WONDER (DEPARTURE) c) I'M A MARIONETTE

Even before it was released, 'The Album' was certain to be ABBA's biggest British success to date, as advance orders had exceeded £1,000,000, which guaranteed it immediate platinum status. Not unexpectedly, it entered the chart at Number One, and remained there for nine weeks, in a Top 10 run of over six months. As most critics noted, 'The Album' was something of a progression for ABBA: while the first side contained four fairly straightforward songs (although all were somewhat longer than the majority of ABBA's material, each clocking in at over four minutes), side two contained the three excerpts from the 'mini-musical', 'The Girl With The Golden Hair'. The vast majority of critics were very negative in their view of this side. *Melody Maker* called the mini-musical "a mistake" and *Record Mirror* decreed "this is where they come horribly unstuck." *Rolling Stone* magazine was more constructive, their reviewer noting: "Side two is a real attempt to do something different, and, if not everything works, the effort is still laudable."

Few would dispute that the first side of 'The Album' is the more rewarding, containing as it does a pair of chart topping singles in 'The Name Of The Game' and 'Take A Chance On Me', the latter spotlighting Agnetha on lead vocals, and the former featuring solo passages from both girls. These two are well-known, of course, but should not be allowed to overshadow either 'Eagle' or 'One Man, One Woman', the tracks which complete the side. Both seem to reflect the influence of Californian country-rock, under whose spell Benny and Björn had fallen at this stage. 'Eagle', as nearly every reviewer noted, appears to be a tribute to The Eagles, the most successful country-rock group of all, but one whose record sales, ironically, are still many millions behind those of ABBA. *New Musical Express* described this track as "a superbly crafted pastiche of The Eagles' style, exactly capturing that sense of clinical blandness," although it would be only fair to note that their reviewer seems to have liked neither ABBA nor The Eagles. In point of fact, 'One Man, One Woman' actually seems closer to country music than 'Eagle', and it is not difficult to imagine Anni-Frid's lead vocal being duplicated by the Queen of country music, Tammy Wynette, of 'Stand By Your Man' fame. In short, side one of 'The Album' is magnificent, although it cannot be denied that side two is very different from anything ABBA had attempted on their previous three albums. 'Move On' starts with a spoken passage by Björn, which was likened by nearly every critic to Wink Martindale's woebegone 'Deck Of Cards', but fortunately improves dramatically when Agnetha's lead vocal begins. 'Hole In Your Soul' is much more energetic, its hard-rocking intro provoking *Melody Maker's* Harry Doherty to draw comparisons with the work of Thin Lizzy, although several reviewers were critical of the lyrics, which they considered simplistic.

The mini-musical begins with one of the most genuinely melodic songs ever composed by ABBA, 'Thank You For The Music', on which Agnetha shines as lead singer. However, the song failed to satisfy critics from several newspapers, notably *New Musical Express,* who called it "the sort of tear jerker that turns up in provincial pantomimes" – a judgement that cannot be easily brushed aside, as it is considerably less rock-orientated than almost anything else ABBA recorded. Conversely, 'I Wonder' (sung by Anni-Frid) and 'I'm A Marionette' feature less tuneful melody lines, although both possess a sense of drama appropriate to the story line.

Of course, by the time 'The Album' was available for review, well over 200,000 copies had passed over record shop counters, which rendered much of the criticism academic. Even so, *New Musical Express* summed up by suggesting that the album "could turn out to be ABBA's least satisfactory" and *Melody Maker* seemed to agree, noting that it was "probably ABBA's weakest album since they hit the big time." Not that it made any difference – especially in America, where 'The Album' was also certified platinum.

(Above and opposite) From the BBC *Snowtime Special*

January 27th, 1978
TAKE A CHANCE ON ME/I'M A MARIONETTE
(Epic EPC 5950)

Despite its inclusion on 'The Album', this became ABBA's seventh British chart-topping single, entering the lists within a week of release, and reaching Number One two weeks later, when it replaced 'Figaro', by ABBA copyists Brotherhood Of Man. In their album review, *New Musical Express* singled out 'Take A Chance On Me' as "one of those unstoppable eighteen line chorus songs which hold the secret of ABBA's success," and in normal circumstances, it would probably have reigned supreme for longer than it did. However, after three weeks, it was prematurely deposed by Kate Bush's stunning debut, 'Wuthering Heights'.

On February 16th, *ABBA – The Movie* was premièred at London's Warner West End cinema before its general release, enabling all ABBA's fans to see the quartet on the silver screen, if not in the flesh. Initially, it was to have been a simple documentary about the 1977 world tour, but after due consideration, it was decided to incorporate a storyline to add interest and excitement. In fact not all the members of ABBA were overjoyed at the prospect of concerts being filmed: Benny was extremely dubious, primarily because of regrettable experiences in the days of The Hep Stars, but after seeing some of the early footage, he was the first to admit that his caution had been unnecessary. Anni-Frid, on the other hand, was very enthusiastic about the entire project, having actually auditioned for film roles in the past, albeit without success, while Agnetha had enjoyed a certain amount of acting experience as Mary in *Jesus Christ Superstar*. Björn, the ultimate professional, was less concerned – as long as the film enhanced ABBA's career, it was all right with him...

The interwoven story was described by the feminist *Spare Rib* magazine as "the worst thing about the film," although their reviewer was perhaps missing the point: the idea was to provide something else besides the group's live performances and scenes back-stage. To add an element of humour and continuity, director Lasse Hallstrom devised an essentially simple plot centring on a disc jockey from a radio station in Sydney, Australia, who is assigned to secure an exclusive in-depth interview with ABBA. The disc jockey, Ashley, who has never done anything like this before, starts by discovering everything he can about ABBA... but then encounters a stumbling block: he has no idea how to approach the group, or who to ask for permission to interview them, and his early attempts inevitably result in failure. This, of course, adds to the tension as Ashley will lose his job if he doesn't succeed in his quest. He follows the group around Australia and, after many days of fruitless attempts, finally comes face to face with them. What happens at this point is the climax of the film – it would be unkind to reveal the ending in case anyone reading this book hasn't seen it.

The cast list is a fairly short one – ABBA play themselves, of course, as does Stig Anderson, while Ashley is played by Australian comedy actor Robert Hughes. Apart from the members of ABBA's backing group, who also play themselves, the only other major parts are those of a bodyguard and the manager of Ashley's radio station, which are taken by Tom Oliver and Bruce Barry, respectively. The executive producers of the film were Stig Anderson and Australian film producer Reg Grundy, whose name should be very familiar to many television viewers, as he is the man responsible for the immensely successful *Neighbours*...

Naturally, ABBA's music is featured strongly throughout *The Movie*, with each of their five albums represented. From 'Waterloo' come the title track and 'Ring Ring', and from the 'ABBA' album, 'S.O.S.', 'Rock Me', 'Mamma Mia', 'I've Been Waiting For You', 'So Long' and 'Intermezzo No.1' (although the last of these may be rather different from the recorded version). From 'Greatest Hits' come 'He Is Your Brother' and 'Fernando', while 'The Album' is represented by 'Hole In Your Soul', 'Name Of The Game', 'I'm A Marionette', 'Eagle' and 'Thank You For The Music'. More interesting, perhaps, is that among the 25 pieces of music featured in the film are five which were not released by ABBA on record.

Two of these are Swedish folk songs, 'Johan Pa Snippen' and 'Polkan Gar', and a third is 'Stoned', another adaption of a traditional tune. The other two are original songs written by Benny and Björn, although neither are likely to appear on record, 'Please Change Your Mind' because it's an instrumental, and 'Get On The Carousel' because, as Björn noted, he and Benny have "stolen" parts of it for subsequent songs. Initially, 'Get On The Carousel' was intended as the fourth song in the 'Girl With The Golden Hair' cycle: as *Melody Maker* noted, "it's a rousing rocker that would have injected sorely-needed life into 'The Album'." Eventually, of course, it wasn't included, and joins 'I Am An A', a song which was used to introduce the individual members of the group on the 1977 tour, as a familiar, but unrecorded ABBA track.

Despite the group's phenomenal success, reviews of *ABBA – The Movie* were almost unanimously critical. *The Sunday People*, for instance, said "one forgets that this is virtually a 90 minute commercial... the overwhelming likeableness of ABBA is astutely rammed home," and *The Guardian* reported "Everything is fine about ABBA except the film they have made. It is awful." The music papers were no more kind: *Sounds* noted: "*The Movie* falls into nearly every trap ever laid for rock bands who attempt to cast their image upon the silver screen," while *New Musical Express* were more savage: "This full-blown epic is shockingly bad, providing the ABBA fan with an embarrassingly feeble plot-line to offset the preponderance of ABBA music." Apparently, it was the story (or perhaps the lack of a substantial story) which most reviewers saw as the film's weakness. From other points of view, it was regarded as something of a triumph: *Radio & Record News* called the photography "superb," and felt that the 'dream sequence', where Ashley dreams he is having a picnic with ABBA, was "brilliantly executed in every aspect of its cinematography."

Lasse Hallstrom explained some of the techniques he used, noting in particular the problems associated with a scene where the group are photographed moving through a 'hall of mirrors' and another where they sing 'Eagle' in a lift, for which he had to invent

completely new filming apparatus. *ABBA – The Movie* also contains the first use of a lighting effect produced by a device known as a 'flutter box', which was actually conceived for the film *Superman*, but was used first by ABBA.

In general, however, more abuse than praise was heaped on *ABBA – The Movie* and a lesser group might have been crushed by the harsh treatment – but at the end of 1978, statistics showed the film to have been the seventh biggest box-office success of the year, following such acknowledged winners as *Star Wars, Grease* and *Saturday Night Fever,* and significantly beating other acclaimed films like *Annie Hall, The Stud* and *The Goodbye Girl*.

ABBA's four day visit to launch the film in Britain was packed with activity: apart from the première, the group were presented with the Carl Allen Songwriting Award by Princess Margaret, were interviewed by BBC Radio One disc jockey Dave Lee Travis, appeared on several TV shows, and spoke to the press. The première also drew several other famous pop stars, including Pete Townshend, John Entwistle and Keith Moon of The Who, Biddu, two members of the New Hearts (who later became Secret Affair) and Connie Booth, ex-wife of John Cleese and his co-star in the highly successful TV show, *Fawlty Towers*.

The press conference, however, was where the most interesting news was revealed: both Anni-Frid and Agnetha intimated that they were preparing for the time when ABBA would no longer be a group. Anni-Frid said "I'm working very hard on preparing for a solo career. I have singing lessons every day, and dancing lessons and fitness sessions three times a week," and she also told journalists that her ambition was to sing in opera. Agnetha admitted that she was very keen on pursuing an acting career, although she had already turned down one film part because she considered it too sexy. Björn also recounted the story of the house in which he and Agnetha had lived before moving to a quieter district of Stockholm to gain more privacy: "We can't sell it because no-one can afford it, so we've had to rent it out to the Norwegian Embassy!"

February 17th, 1978
WATERLOO/WATCH OUT (Epic EPC 5961)
FERNANDO/HEY, HEY, HELEN (Epic EPC 5962)

What? Reissues? But surely the originals were still available through any reasonably aware record shop? Hugh Attwooll and Malcolm Eade of CBS/Epic International A&R Department cleared up the confusion: they were re-issued in re-designed picture sleeves as part of a special series of 20 Number One singles. But why select this particular pair from all ABBA's chart toppers? "'Waterloo' was their first Number One, and 'Fernando' was their biggest in sales terms." So now we know... but neither of them were hits second time round, probably because everyone already had them!

After the international launch of *The Movie*, ABBA retreated to Stockholm, where Björn and Benny got back into the song-writing routine, while Agnetha spent most of her time with her children, and Anni-Frid continued with her singing and dancing lessons. It was time for all four to return to being normal people for a while. Stig Anderson, meanwhile, was planning for the future, with particular reference to the United States. "By and large, the US still remains for us to conquer. We've racked up good sales over the past few years – our albums get into the Top 40, and some of the singles have done even better than that, like 'Dancing Queen', which was Number One, but we still haven't broken down the heaviest doors, so to speak. To be frank, we're not the household name over there we'd like to be."

There's no doubt that success is most pleasing when it's won in the face of strong odds. By this time in their career, ABBA had very little to aim for in most other countries apart from equalling their previous achievements. After all, when you've reached Number One as often as ABBA, getting there again isn't really progress, but more a question of consolidation, and not losing ground. The only country of any significance which wasn't totally under their spell was America.

It wasn't as if they hadn't been trying to incorporate the United States into the ABBA empire, they just hadn't broken through, so obviously a fresh line of attack was needed. Stig decided to hire the famous American 'starmakers', Scotti Brothers, whose previous clients had included Barbra Streisand, John Denver and Leif Garrett. Their first move was to make May 1978 *ABBA Month* in America, and to arrange for the group to appear as special guests in a TV special which starred their old friend Olivia Newton-John, who had climbed to superstardom since being beaten by ABBA in the 1974 Eurovision Song Contest. Apart from winning three Grammy awards and numerous gold and platinum records, Olivia had also become extremely popular as a result of her starring role in the film *Grease* with John Travolta, and she was then one of the most celebrated singers in the world – especially in America, where she had taken up residence. For ABBA to appear on a nationally networked show with Olivia would certainly attract maximum attention, but the groundwork laid during *ABBA Month* was equally important, involving spectacular window displays in record shops around America, plus as many localised TV and radio appearances as possible. Perhaps the single most exciting aspect of this rigorous publicity campaign was a giant billboard overlooking Sunset Strip in Los Angeles – anyone whose record company foots the bill for this extravagance is expected to recoup the investment at some speed!

Added to all this activity was nationwide TV advertising for 'The Album' and a major promotional push on their latest US single, 'Take A Chance On Me'. ABBA's American record label, Atlantic, considered them to have more unrealised potential than any other act on their roster, but even after this deluge of publicity (Stig estimated that nearly $1 million was lavished during this concerted effort to convert America), ABBA must have been somewhat disappointed. Not that the eventual chart peak of 'The Album' (as high as No.14, or as low as No.33, depending on which trade paper's chart you were reading) or the Top 10 position of 'Take A Chance On Me' were bad, it was just that they could have been so much better. In fact, 'The Album' was their most successful LP to date, while 'Take A Chance On Me' equalled the sales of 'Waterloo', whose chart position had only been bettered by 'Dancing Queen' in all their four years of American attack.

Back in Britain, ABBA continued to devastate previous records: during May, it was announced that 'The Album' had already been certified triple platinum for sales of more than £3,000,000 and on June 12th, a record dealer in Reading was presented with the one millionth copy of 'The Album' by the Sales Director of CBS Records. Also in May, ABBA's own recording studio, Polar, was completed. It was certainly the most technically advanced recording facility in Sweden, and possibly in the whole of Europe, with 48 track capability and just about every recording sophistication invented at the time. Obviously, ABBA intended to be its primary customers (rather than returning to Metronome or Glen Studios, where they had recorded before) but, when their commitments allowed, the premises could be used by other artists. Among those who took advantage of this during the studio's first 18 months were Led Zeppelin, who recorded their highly successful 1979 come-back album, 'In Through The Out Door', at Polar, and Genesis members Tony Banks and Mike Rutherford, who each made solo albums there.

During the summer of 1978, ABBA took a seven week holiday, their first real break since leaving school many years before. Of course, about half the tracks for the next ABBA album had to be completed before Björn and Benny, in particular, could spend such a long time away from work with a clear conscience. Meanwhile, Agnetha was presented with a songwriting award by the Swedish Society of Popular Music Composers, and Benny and Anni-Frid took delivery of a new boat, which they sailed along the Baltic coast at the start of July. During August, Phil McNeill, assistant editor of *New Musical Express*, flew to Stockholm to interview ABBA. This particular publication was not noted for its generosity when reporting on the type of music made by ABBA, but nevertheless some interesting information resulted from McNeill's lengthy feature. He established that, apart from ABBA, the Polar Records artist roster included Svenne & Lotta, Lena Andersson and Ted Gardestad, all of whom have been mentioned before, but also a lady singer named Birgitta Wollgard, described as sounding similar to Bonnie Tyler, and (Lasse) Wellander & (Mats) Ronander, "a studio rock supergroup." (McNeill was under the impression that none of these acts had records released in Britain, although in fact Ted Gardestad has had several British releases, notably his 'Blue Virgin Isles' album, most of which was recorded in Los Angeles). It was also discovered that by this time, many of the ABBA lyrics which had previously been written by Stig Anderson were now being created by Björn, as Stig was devoting almost all his working hours to managerial and administrative duties. Perhaps the most interesting point raised by McNeill was his conclusion that many parallels existed between ABBA and The Bee Gees. While several of his observations seemed correct – for example, the fact that both groups had experienced bad times before finally coming out on top – other comparisons appeared to have been motivated by the problems McNeill had experienced in talking to the group, something he shared with 'Ashley' in *The Movie*. Among these were the assertions that neither group possessed any personality, and that neither could write "a decent lyric to save its life." Nevertheless, it was one of the more thoughtful articles written about ABBA.

ABBA
SUMMER NIGHT CITY

September 8th, 1978
SUMMERNIGHT CITY/MEDLEY: PICK A BALE OF COTTON/ON TOP OF OLD SMOKEY/MIDNIGHT SPECIAL
(Epic EPC 6595)

It had been a long time since 'Take A Chance On Me' had topped the chart, but ABBA's British fans had not forgotten about them, as brisk sales indicated. However, 'Summer Night City' peaked at No.5, becoming the quartet's first single not to make the Top 3 in nearly three years, and most reviewers were appalled to note that the A side seemed to be powered by an unmistakable disco beat. When asked about this, Björn said "Everyone's doing it – it's the pulse of the '70s," although such an obvious answer was ill-received by critics: *Record Mirror* wrote "the calculating Swedes have produced a piece of disco muzak," *New Musical Express* said "ABBA go disco – the song's by no means as memorable as earlier stuff," and *Melody Maker*, reinforcing a general feeling that ABBA were strongly influenced by The Bee Gees at this time, decided "It was only a matter of time before they sidled into the Gibb Brothers' disco penthouse." It was also *Melody Maker* which printed a gossip item alleging that at the end of 'Summer Night City', the words "love making love in the moonlight" appeared, although most listeners have agreed that this is conjecture, as it is difficult to hear with any clarity what is being sung as the record fades to a close.

The B side of the single is another ABBA curiosity, a medley of three traditional folk songs recorded in 1975, and previously released only in Germany on a charity album titled 'Die Deutsche Krebshilfe', which also featured several other artists. The middle song of the three, 'On Top Of Old Smokey', showcases Anni-Frid's lead vocals, while the other two feature duets. No doubt the medley was an affectionate backward glance at Björn's days as a Hootenanny Singer.

ABBA 初来日記者会見

ウッラ ウーデバル
Mrs. ULLA M. ○DEFALL

ベンクト ウーデバル
H.E. Mr. BENGT ○DEFALL

ビヨルン
BJÖRN ULVAEUS

アンナ
AGNETHA FÄLTSKOG

フリーダ
ANNIFRID LYNGSTAD

ベニー
BENNY ANDERSSON

Following the release of the single, the group returned to the studio with the intention of completing their next album in time for the Christmas market, although, as it turned out, this proved to be an optimistic deadline. While they were ensconced in the studio during September, Agnetha undertook a telephone interview with *The Sun*, in which she intimated that ABBA might not perform live again, saying "It's such a lot of trouble to go on the road, and I've no intention of letting my children be brought up by somebody else. The family must come first." After being presented with a gold disc for sales of 'The Album' in France, ABBA interrupted their recording schedule for a mid-October appearance on a French TV show, but prior to that, on October 6th, the inevitable event occurred: Benny and Anni-Frid finally got married after living together for nine years. The ceremony was conducted in some secrecy at their local church, with very few other people present, the witnesses being a churchwarden and the couple's house-keeper. As Benny said afterwards, 'It had to be a quiet ceremony, because we didn't want it to be like Björn and Agnetha's wedding where there were so many people that it was just too crowded. Not that we didn't want our fans to know about it, but we both felt that our wedding was very personal, and we didn't want it spoiled by anything like that."

November found ABBA in Japan, where they recorded a one hour TV special for the Tokyo Broadcasting System, after three other TV shows, including the *Olivia Newton-John Special*, had been shown in Japan during the year, resulting in three of their albums appearing simultaneously in the Japanese Top 20. On the way to Japan, the group stopped off briefly in Hollywood, where their appearance on the world famous *Dick Clark Show* pleasantly coincided with both 'Greatest Hits' and 'The Album' achieving platinum status in the United States.

Following such successful trips to two of the world's biggest record-buying markets, ABBA had only a few days at home before they were off again, this time to Britain, to record a Christmas TV show hosted by Mike Yarwood and a slot for Jimmy Saville's

Jim'll Fix It programme. More important were the announcements of two other TV shows being set up for the early part of 1978: The Bee Gees' UNICEF gala concert to be held in New York, and the one hour *Snowtime Special*, which would be specially filmed by the BBC during February. On a lighter (and ultra-hygienic) note to end the year, a product known as 'ABBA – The Soap' went on sale – as *Record Mirror* noted, "You too can be as clean as the Scandinavian sauna freaks... and all for 49p!"

1978 seemed to have been a perfect year, when everything had gone very well for the members of ABBA. But despite outside appearances, a shadow had been looming, on Christmas Eve 1978, Agnetha and Björn decided to separate, and Agnetha moved out of their house. Perhaps now that bizarre picture, which 21 months previously had graced the sleeve of the 'Greatest Hits' album, was starting to make sense.

The beginning of 1979 saw Stig Anderson summoning all his vast experience to avert the potential disaster which could so easily have resulted from the break up of Björn and Agnetha's marriage. Although he had not encountered this particular problem before, there was probably no-one better equipped to deal with it than Stig: apart from his obvious close ties with ABBA, he had been a successful part of the world's music industry for 20 years, since starting Sweden Music in 1960, the company of which Polar Music was originally a subsidiary. It was Stig who had suggested the name ABBA for his quartet of prodigies. As well as piloting them through their formative years (and contributing lyrics to many of their best known songs), it was Stig who had conceived the strategy of signing ABBA to different record companies around the world, and who had helped them invest their vast earnings to ensure the greatest possible financial security. Whatever happened, there would be no need for any of the ABBA quartet – nor Stig, for that matter – ever to work again, but if everything were to stop dead because of a divorce, all five would regret having failed to reach their full potential as the world's most successful group.

Not that ABBA's musical future was Stig's only concern; he had known Björn and Agnetha almost since they were teenagers, and was undoubtedly very upset that their marriage had encountered stormy weather... but it often seems that when two people have grown apart to the extent of Agnetha and Björn, the only way they can recover their happiness is to cease living together, which is what they did.

One of ABBA's principal virtues had always been their reliability (as Stig told one journalist, "If we promise something, we keep our promise. It's hard sometimes, but I very much believe in this"), and during the first weeks of 1979, they had promised to perform in a very special show. Described by one British critic as "the greatest pop show ever to be seen on television," the event was to be hosted by The Bee Gees at the General Assembly Hall of the United Nations in New York, and all proceeds were to be

1979
KEEPING IT TOGETHER

donated to the United Nations Childrens Fund, UNICEF, in recognition of *The Year Of The Child*. After keeping so many less important promises to comparatively minor causes, it would obviously be quite wrong for ABBA to break this one...

Of course, it wasn't the first time divorced show business personalities had continued to work together – a prime example was John and Christine McVie, whose matrimonial upset did not impinge on their professional relationship as colleagues in one of ABBA's favourite groups, Fleetwood Mac – and fortunately, Björn and Agnetha elected to follow suit, taking little time to work out that there was no need for their private tragedy to affect their best friends. They made this clear in a joint statement to the world's press during 1979: "We just couldn't live together any longer, and we're filing for divorce. When you talk about everything and still fail to get through to each other, then you must take the consequences. We just grew apart." Björn added "This is a friendly separation, if such a thing exists, and there is no reason for ABBA to stop performing as a group." Of course, this prompted numerous newspaper features deprecating married couples who were in the habit of "working, as well as sleeping, side by side." "It's an old rule," said one, "that marriage and work don't mix, because a couple working in the same office can easily put their domestic problems before efficiency."

A few days after the marital problems had been revealed to the press, Stig, apparently relieved that the situation had been brought into the open, told the *Daily Express*: "The divorce had been on the cards for a year. Now they have made the decision, they are a lot happier, but before, they couldn't make up their minds to do one thing or another." Of course, 1978 had been ABBA's least prolific year since they rose to fame, and while the imminent arrival and subsequent birth of Christian had been highly significant factors in that lack of activity, it could hardly be denied that the group's output had slowed to a trickle...

On January 8th, 1979, ABBA arrived in New York for the UNICEF gala, an occasion which showcased ten of the biggest pop acts in the world. Apart from ABBA and The Bee Gees, the line-up was to include Olivia Newton-John, Andy Gibb (the younger brother of the Bee Gees), Rod Stewart, Kris Kristofferson & Rita Coolige, Barry Manilow and Elton John, but by the time of the concert which was compèred by David Frost, Henry 'Fonzie' Winkler and Gilda Radner, Messrs. John and Manilow had dropped out, to be replaced by Donna Summer, John Denver and Earth, Wind & Fire. Inevitably, the event was a

staggering success, and was filmed for later showing on television in more than 70 countries, attracting an estimated audience of more than 300 million people!
As well as refusing any payment, each act donated the royalties from one of their songs to UNICEF, and the eventual proceeds were expected to exceed £50,000,000. All in all, the event constituted a remarkably successful fund-raising effort "to provide food, health care, shelter and education for needy children in 100 developing countries around the globe."

A week after the UNICEF concert, the *Daily Mail* published a feature examining some of the unusual methods of payment which top rock stars found acceptable. American singer Bette Midler, it was revealed, received gold bullion for a European tour, while Boney M, after their concerts in Russia, took a substantial percentage of their payment in furs. Predictably, ABBA's business dealings did not escape scrutiny: as previously mentioned Stig was said to have negotiated a deal whereby royalties from records sold in the communist bloc of Eastern Europe were paid in oil, and even in potatoes! A few days later, another paper confirmed Russian interest in ABBA, when it reported that police were required to control crowds who had queued for several hours in temperatures many degrees below freezing, after a small consignment of ABBA albums had been put on sale by a Moscow record store. Although the shop sold out before lunchtime, many fans continued queueing in the vain hope of fresh supplies materialising, and eventually police were called in to quell the growing unrest.

January 26th, 1979
CHIQUITITA/LOVELIGHT (Epic EPC 7030)

After a gap of more than four months, and with the shock of the divorce still fresh in their minds, the British public were obviously still very eager to buy a new single from ABBA, especially as it introduced their new – and as yet unfinished album. Within a week of release, 'Chiquitita', with lead vocal by Agnetha, entered the chart at No.8, but was unable to displace Blondie's 'Heart Of Glass' from the head of the list, although it did reach No.2 for two weeks of its nine week chart residency. As one critic noted, it was somewhat reminiscent of 'Fernando', "with atmospheric Spanish guitars playing," and,

(Below) Frida and Agnetha on stage at Wembley Arena – World Tour 1979

incidentally, was the song which ABBA had chosen to donate to the UNICEF cause. 'Lovelight', combining lead vocals by both girls, increased the growing list of ABBA recordings unavailable on an album, prompting one or two critics to suggest the release of a compilation album which collected all such tracks.

February saw ABBA back in Sweden, where Benny and Björn were adding the final touches to the new album. They had already spent some time in the Bahamas, and later in Miami, Florida, writing songs and trying out American recording studios, but ultimately they chose to record almost the entire album at Polar Studios in Stockholm. Anni-Frid, meanwhile, worked to improve her dancing and singing techniques, while Agnetha laid the foundations to a new life without her husband. Stig flew to Cannes to attend MIDEM, the international music business convention, where he told newsmen that ABBA would be embarking on their first tours of Canada and the USA later in the year. Additionally, he confirmed that both 'Arrival' and 'The Album' would be released (rather than imported) in Russia, where an ABBA TV special was also due to be screened, and he revealed that the group's appearance on Japanese television during the previous December had resulted in sales in Japan of over 800,000 copies within one month!

The next item on the agenda was a trip to Leysin in Switzerland, where the group were to be filmed for a BBC-TV spectacular in the *Snowtime Special* series – to be called, logically enough, *ABBA In Switzerland*, and to be screened over Easter in a number of European countries. (The programme also included guest appearances by Kate Bush and Roxy Music). ABBA performed a number of their familiar hits plus two songs from their forthcoming album: 'The King Has Lost His Crown' and 'Kisses Of Fire'.

Not unnaturally, a good deal of the accompanying media attention centred on the impending divorce, and several British newspapers published major pictorial stories on the subject, as well as trying to fuel a scandal (where none apparently existed) over Björn's alleged alliance with Liz Mitchell, one of the members of Boney M, who were also in Leysin filming a *Snowtime Special*. The dissolution of a celebrated marriage is always a cue for gossip columnists to generate what are known as 'factoids', a term used to describe events which may not have happened, but which have been written about so much that a large number of people believe them to be true. One such factoid concerned Agnetha. When the marriage began to disintegrate, she and Björn had consulted a psychiatrist named Hakan Lonnback, and it was alleged that he had left his family to live with Agnetha, although she firmly denied these rumours. Ironically, although few people knew it at the time, it was Björn who had found a new lover: "I lived a bachelor life for only one week," he admitted when the world found out about his new paramour, 30 year old Lena Kallersjo.

On their homecoming from Switzerland, Benny and Björn returned to the studio to mix and master the new album, while Anni-Frid made a significant move towards realising her ambitions: she accepted a part in a Swedish film titled *Walk On Water If You Can*, which was subsequently filmed on location in Spain. Ironically, in view of the recent traumas afflicting ABBA, she played the part of a wife experiencing problems in her love life. As she said at the time, "Although it's a small part, I feel it could lead to better things. I'm enjoying it, but no, I've no intention of abandoning my singing career."

It was also announced at this time that ABBA would be expanding their projected tour schedule to take in much of Europe as well as the Americas, although this time they were not planning to visit Australia, and as soon as the album and Frida's film part were safely in the can, the group began serious rehearsals for their live appearances. April 1979 saw the screening of *ABBA In Switzerland*. As usual, there was much discussion over the BBC's decision to feature ABBA although few people were aware that all the performers in the show – ABBA, Roxy Music, Kate Bush and Ted Gardestad – had waived their fees in favour of a donation to UNICEF. Although inevitably the critics were not unanimous in their praise, the general consensus of opinion was one of approval, and might be summed up by a critic who wrote "*ABBA In Switzerland* made staying at home in front of the box a real pleasure."

April 27th, 1979
DOES YOUR MOTHER KNOW/KISSES OF FIRE
(Epic EPC 7316)

Both sides of the new single came from the imminent 'Voulez-Vous' album, and 'Does Your Mother Know', which was unveiled in *ABBA In Switzerland*, was a track which had excited a certain amount of criticism when it was first heard on television but was still unanimously predicted a hit. It was, of course, entering the chart eight days after release, and remaining there for nine weeks, in the course of which it peaked at No.4. For the first time since the group's rise to superstardom, Björn was lead singer on the A side of an ABBA single, and the change came as rather a surprise to some critics. One likened the track to something which might have been recorded by The Rolling Stones, while another noted that the single also contained the rare sound (for ABBA records) of a stridently blown saxophone. Perhaps the lack of lead vocals by the girls was what prevented 'Does Your Mother Know' from reaching the Top 3 (or above), but 'Kisses Of Fire' might have redressed the balance, being much more recognisably ABBA in that it featured the lead voice of Agnetha.

May 4th 1979
VOULEZ-VOUS (LP) (Epic EPC 86086)
Side One: AS GOOD AS NEW/VOULEZ-VOUS/I HAVE A DREAM/
ANGELEYES/THE KING HAS LOST HIS CROWN
Side Two: DOES YOUR MOTHER KNOW/IF IT WASN'T FOR THE NIGHTS/
CHIQUITITA/LOVERS (LIVE A LITTLE LONGER)/KISSES OF FIRE

It had been 15 months since the release of 'The Album', but it was still buoyant in the album charts when 'Voulez-Vous' was released. Advance orders were predictably heavy, and the new album shot immediately to Number One, equalling the achievement of 'The Album', but remaining in the top position for rather less time, four weeks, as opposed to its predecessor's nine. During its first week in the shops, sales exceeding 400,000 bestowed instant platinum status in Britain, making it the fastest selling ABBA album to date and completely justifying their bold changes of musical direction.

Eventually, seven of the album's ten tracks were released in single form, and five of these appeared in the hit parade, a feat which recalled the equally high overall standard of the 'ABBA' album. This time, however, the group had allowed themselves room to expand: three of the tracks each lasted over five minutes, two others over four minutes, and none was shorter than three minutes. Not unexpectedly, the songs had taken much longer to write than the material for any previous album, partly because Stig Anderson no longer had the time to assist lyrically and, perhaps more importantly, because of the depth of emotion displayed in their subject matter. Where early songs had been comparatively shallow and rarely bitter, the songs on 'Voulez-Vous' were much more adult, frequently dealing with more mature stages of love, and the potential problems which can arise, and this new approach to writing was seen as a desire for the group to be taken more seriously.

Musically, the major change was the prominent contribution by Janne Schaffer, the lead guitarist who had worked with ABBA earlier in their career and who had now become

recognised as a gifted jazz artist. He was featured on those tracks with the most insistent disco beat, while the others, featuring regular guitarist Lasse Wellander, were closer to ABBA's previous sound. Other innovations included the use of inventive string passages (arranged either by bass player Rutger Gunnarsson or Anders Eljas, who would both join ABBA's touring party later in the year) and the adoption of a basic rhythm track (for the title song) recorded as an experiment at Criteria Studios in Miami, where The Bee Gees make their records, with help from noted American producer Tom Dowd, who had been responsible for supervising such big selling and very familiar classic hits as 'Layla' and 'I Shot The Sheriff' for Eric Clapton, and 'Sailing' and 'The First Cut Is The Deepest' for Rod Stewart.

Obviously, any anxiety that Björn and Benny might have felt about the acceptability of their more mature approach was soon dispelled by the album's colossal success. One interesting side issue was that Buddy McCluskey, who worked for RCA Records, Polar's Argentinian licensees, wrote a set of Spanish lyrics for 'Chiquitita'. The group re-recorded their vocals, and the modified single was released in the Spanish-speaking world, becoming an instant smash hit all over South America and topping the charts in Argentina, Chile, Colombia, Ecuador, El Salvador, Panama, Peru and Venezuela. In many of these countries, the English version of the song also reached the Top 5, while 'Voulez-Vous' topped the album charts almost everywhere in a continent not previously considered a major record selling market for European or American artists.
At the end of May, this great interest shown in the quartet by the Spanish-speaking world resulted in ABBA making a TV special in Madrid, Spain, where they were able to perform the Spanish version of 'Chiquitita' as well as other songs in English. Stig, meanwhile, spent some time in North America, working on arrangements for the upcoming tour. Although 'Chiquitita' had not been released in the United States, 'Does Your Mother

Know' was making very encouraging upward movements, and would eventually reach the Top 20 in all three American trade charts, despite not being especially typical of what ABBA did best...

It was also announced that members of ABBA's fan club would be allowed to reserve tickets for the group's British concerts scheduled for November. This would effectively prevent their more committed followers from having to be involved in the flood of applications expected after the group's previous tour when, you may recall, more than three and a half million ticket applications were received. It was an expensive month for ABBA fans – apart from the new album and forthcoming concerts, few female fans would have wanted to be without two newly-marketed cologne fragrances, which had been named after the girls in the group. Agnetha's perfume, called Anna, was described as "light, fresh and floral, and designed for daytime use," while Anni-Frid's, called Frida, was "warm and spicy and made for evening use."

THE MUSIC FOR UNICEF CONCERT/A GIFT OF SONG
(LP) (Polydor 2335 214)
Side One: SEPTEMBER/THAT'S THE WAY OF THE WORLD (Earth, Wind & Fire)/I GO FOR YOU (Andy Gibb)/MIMI'S SONG (Donna Summer)/
REST YOUR LOVE ON ME (Andy Gibb & Olivia Newton-John)/
CHIQUITITA (ABBA)
Side Two: DA YA THINK I'M SEXY (Rod Stewart)/THE KEY (Olivia Newton-John)/RHYMES AND REASONS (John Denver)/FALLEN ANGELS (Kris Kristofferson & Rita Coolidge)/TOO MUCH HEAVEN (Bee Gees)

A more star-studded album would be hard to imagine! Recorded at the UNICEF gala in New York earlier in the year, it featured a high percentage of the biggest stars in the world at the time. According to eye witness reports, however, it was hardly an accurate representation of the music made that evening. For example, the chance to hear duets between Rod Stewart and Kris Kristofferson or between Donna Summer and Rita Coolidge could have been fascinating. Also, while several of the songs on the album (including 'Chiquitita') were donated to the UNICEF cause, this was not true of everything on the record. Obviously, 'Chiquitita' is of particular interest, but in truth, it is little more than a very accurate live performance of the song, differing from the more familiar version only in that it is somewhat shorter (the long instrumental ending is faded almost as soon as it begins), that the sound of the audience clapping along can be heard, and that the performance seems to lack the polish of the original.

One very good reason to own this album is that it benefits a worthy cause, and also completes any collection of ABBA records. However, it seems that in Britain especially, the record company who released it, conscious, perhaps, of the limited profit accruing from a charity album, did little to publicise its existence. One magazine offered the record as a competition prize, but found it exceedingly difficult to order copies from a record shop, and it seems most peculiar that an album of unique performances by such acclaimed super-stars should have failed to enter the British album chart.

CHIQUITITA FOR CHARITY

July 6th, 1979
ANGELEYES/VOULEZ-VOUS (Epic EPC 7499)

Two more tracks from the 'Voulez-Vous' album, initially released as a double header, but subsequently relaunched as a normal coupling with 'Angeleyes' as the featured side after two confusing weeks in the chart, where it arrived at the strangely low position of No.48 a few days after release. Although it spent 11 weeks in the best sellers, and reached No.3 during the month of August, this was by no means the most successful ABBA single, largely because Roxy Music had also released a single titled 'Angel Eyes', spelt as two words instead of one and a quite different song. Such confusion rarely occurs, but when it does, both acts tend to lose out. Both sides of the single featured Janne

Schaffer, whereas the previous three extracted single tracks from 'Voulez-Vous' had included guitar work by Lasse Wellander: perhaps this release was another part of the experiment to discover whether two comparatively long tracks (totalling more than nine and a half minutes together) would be acceptable to singles buyers. Obviously, there was little need for concern on that score. Producer Tom Dowd explained how he came to be involved with ABBA: "ABBA were impressed with the nature of a pile of records that had come out on Atlantic Records, or the Warner Bros. complex, and they were interested in trying to put together an American rhythm section to try and make demos of several songs of a particular type. They were on holiday in the Bahamas and they called up Atlantic and said they'd like to go to Criteria Studio in Miami to see those rhythm sections and make a record with them. I got back to Miami from California, and my wife said 'ABBA are looking for you, they're up at Criteria right now', so I got back in the car and drove up to the studio. They were running through one or two songs, and trying to experiment with the rhythm section, and I got on the floor and changed the parts and the sequence and everything, and we made a good demo that day, and they wanted to come back the next day and re-work that song and some other things, and we made two tracks for them the next day. They said they'd like to possibly come back and do some more songs with these people, but they didn't have any written – and that was the last we saw of them, until the record came out and we recognised one of the tracks that we had made that they had put things on top of and then finished." Which is how part of 'Voulez-Vous' came to be recorded...

On September 13th, 1979, ABBA launched their first American tour with a concert in Edmonton, Canada. In the course of 18 dates spread over three and a half weeks the group was seen by more than 140,000 people, and each 90 minute show drew a standing ovation, necessitating encores at every gig. Although most of the venues were filled to capacity, there were empty seats in some cities, illustrating that the group had yet to conquer North America as comprehensively as they had the rest of the Western world, but the general critical response was undeniably enthusiastic. The reviews of their shows, despite reservations (hardly surprising, as few Americans had ever seen the group play live before), were encouraging, although not all as positive as the critic who wrote "One thing is for certain – the ABBA explosion is just beginning in the USA." As for the group... well, they felt very pleased to have made such an impression on their first American tour. As Stig commented: "What gives us the most pleasure is that we have proved music can come from anywhere, not just England or North America."

OCTOBER 12th, 1979
GIMME! GIMME! GIMME! (A MAN AFTER MIDNIGHT)/ THE KING HAS LOST HIS CROWN (Epic EPC 7914)

Released during a two week gap in their touring schedule, this single heralded the imminent arrival of the 'Greatest Hits Vol. 2' album. Just as its forerunner, 'Greatest Hits', had optimistically included a brand new track ('Fernando'), 'Vol. 2' carried 'Gimme! Gimme! Gimme!' even though it had been out for less than a month and had only been heard by their American audiences. Dominated by a forceful disco beat, swirling orchestration and Agnetha's zestful lead vocal, it entered the chart as soon as it was available, and remained there for nine weeks, peaking once again at No.3, a position it achieved during the week of the group's British appearances. It was ABBA's fourth hit of the year, more than they had ever previously enjoyed. Even so, their involvement with the 1979 singles chart was not yet over.

On October 19th, 1979, ABBA set off on the second leg of their world tour, visiting Sweden , Denmark, France, Holland, West Germany, Switzerland, Austria and Belgium before concluding with ten dates in Britain, centred around a six day residency at London's Wembley Arena. Anticipation was high: the 48,000 seats available for the Wembley concerts had been sold within hours five months earlier, and tickets had been snapped up just as eagerly for their other British concerts.

Once again, a nine piece backing group had been assembled to replicate the complexities of ABBA's records: four of the musicians, guitarist Lasse Wellander, keyboard player Anders

Eljas and the faithful rhythm section of Ola Brunkert on drums and Rutger Gunnarsson on bass, remained from the previous tour two and a half years before, while the newcomers included another guitarist, Mats Ronander, Ake Sundqvist on keyboards, and a trio of backing singers in Birgitta Wollgard, Liza Ohman and Thomas Ledin. Thomas was himself a Polar Music artist, and was featured performing a song he had written, 'Not Bad At All' – just one of numerous aspects significantly different from the expected formula of reproducing well known hits. Each of the four principals was spotlighted in a solo role, and if Benny and Björn's features were somewhat predictable (although Benny's keyboard ingenuities could hardly have been foreseen), the girls more than made up for it. Anni-Frid's song and dance routines, together with her performance of 'I Have A Dream', incorporating a children's choir (a local choir was provided on every concert during the tour), went down particularly well... but it was Agnetha who stole the show for many ABBA fans, playing and singing one of her own compositions, 'I'm Still Alive', which was especially poignant in view of her impending divorce. While the stage set for their previous tour had been somewhat unremarkable, ABBA's 1979 expedition was memorable for the pyramid-shaped moving backdrop (especially designed and created in England), which added a spectacular touch of magic to the proceedings. So too did the sensational costumes, manufactured from Spandex, a figure-hugging fabric which accentuated the shapely contours of the girls in particular, to great effect! Predictably, ABBA's fans were overwhelmed by the show, but not so the blasé critics, many of whom echoed the sentiments expressed by the *Daily Mail's* Simon Kinnersley, who considered it to have been "one of the most dull and turgid concerts I've attended in months." Garth Pearce of the *Daily Express* headlined his piece "Oh ABBA! What a damp squib for Bonfire Night" (the first night of the Wembley engagement was November 5th), and indeed the vast majority of critics seemed to have been expecting something other than what they saw. Was that their fault – or was it ABBA's?

(Above) 1979 World Tour programme

October 26th, 1979
GREATEST HITS VOL. 2 (LP) (Epic EPC 10017)
Side One: GIMME! GIMME! GIMME! (A MAN AFTER MIDNIGHT)/KNOWING ME, KNOWING YOU/TAKE A CHANCE ON ME/MONEY, MONEY, MONEY/ ROCK ME/EAGLE/ANGELEYES
Side Two: DANCING QUEEN/DOES YOUR MOTHER KNOW/CHIQUITITA/ SUMMER NIGHT CITY/I WONDER (DEPARTURE)/THE NAME OF THE GAME/ THANK YOU FOR THE MUSIC

Released to coincide with the tour, this final ABBA album of the 1970s attracted the amazing total of 600,000 advance orders, thereby guaranteeing double platinum status (for sales exceeding £2,000,000) on the day of release. Strangely, it reached only No.8 in its first week of release (due to Epic Records having been unable to produce sufficient copies to satisfy the incredible demand), but it sprang to Number One the following week, staying there until supplanted by Rod Stewart's 'Greatest Hits' album three weeks later.

At this point, ABBA's first volume of 'Greatest Hits' had sold more than two million copies, while the 'Voulez-Vous' album, also on the way to its second million, was still firmly implanted in the Top 50. With 'The Album' having sold equally well, more than half the tracks on the latest release were already owned by over a million British record buyers, but this did not prevent 'Greatest Hits Volume Two' from selling faster than any previous ABBA album. In fact, no less than 12 of the record's 14 tracks had appeared on an album before, the only exceptions being 'Summer Night City' and 'Gimme! Gimme! Gimme!'. Five tracks came from 'The Album', three each from 'Arrival' and 'Voulez-Vous', while 'Rock Me' was the sole representative of the group's pre-1976 period. Altogether, the album contained the A sides of ten Top 5 singles, and the only curiosity concerns the omission of the title track of the 'Voulez-Vous' album, which had briefly figured in the charts when paired with 'Angeleyes' as a twin-header. Even so, as a CBS press release somewhat inaccurately noted, "With the release of this album, ABBA wind up the '70s in the same way they started – on top." If the decade had started in April, 1974, the comment would have been more accurate, as ABBA didn't even exist as such at the beginning of the 1970s...

Following the concert tour, the ABBA entourage returned to Sweden for a well-earned rest. Agnetha, in particular, was pleased to be back with her children, although a good deal of speculation had been aroused by a rumour indicating that she was thinking of leaving ABBA. Eventually, it transpired that this was not the case – the group would quite definitely continue in its classic formation. However, Agnetha, always the one who least enjoyed touring, announced that she wanted some time away from the group during 1980, especially during the late summer, when Linda would be starting school. As she said, "The first few months at school is when Linda needs me most. I'm as excited as anybody about going on tour, but for me, there is always a little sadness when I think about the children at home."

Backstage at Wembley, I renewed my acquaintance with Björn and Benny, whom I had last talked with a couple of years before. Did Björn feel that ABBA's conquest of the world was now complete? "It depends how you look at it. Most people would say we've conquered the USA because our albums have gone platinum. If you consider the States conquered, then there's nowhere they don't play ABBA, except maybe China – but I don't think they have many record players there! If they had, they'd be playing ABBA."
What about Russia – I gather that the Russians want you to tour there. "Well, we have no plans to perform there at the moment." And will this tour be the last ABBA undertakes? "We're looking at it as a final tour, but we said the same about the last tour. We're not saying it's a farewell tour though, because we've seen The Rolling Stones do that several times. If we're still together, still writing, and we still think it's fun, I'll bet that in two years from now, we'll be touring again."

I asked Benny why this tour had not included concerts in their stronghold of Australia... "Well, one reason is that it's a terribly long flight to Australia – 34 hours on the plane. If you don't feel you have to go there, it's pleasanter to stay at home. Not that we've done a lot of touring – since Brighton, we've only been on the road about 12 weeks in all, and that's not much. I do enjoy tours, but not all the travelling and the hotel rooms, and I certainly prefer the creative side of my work. It's much pleasanter for me to create music in the studio than to just reproduce it on stage."

Both Benny and Björn seemed uncertain as to how long ABBA might be able to continue without circumstances affecting their remarkable stability, which had been unshakeable for around seven years. Benny: "I've no idea how long we can continue. I wouldn't dare to make a guess. It's a matter of will and potential, wanting to do something. But I really enjoy what I do. Without work, life would be meaningless – it's the major part of my life." Björn expressed similar sentiments: "I don't know how much longer we can go on, but we don't make any long range plans any more..."

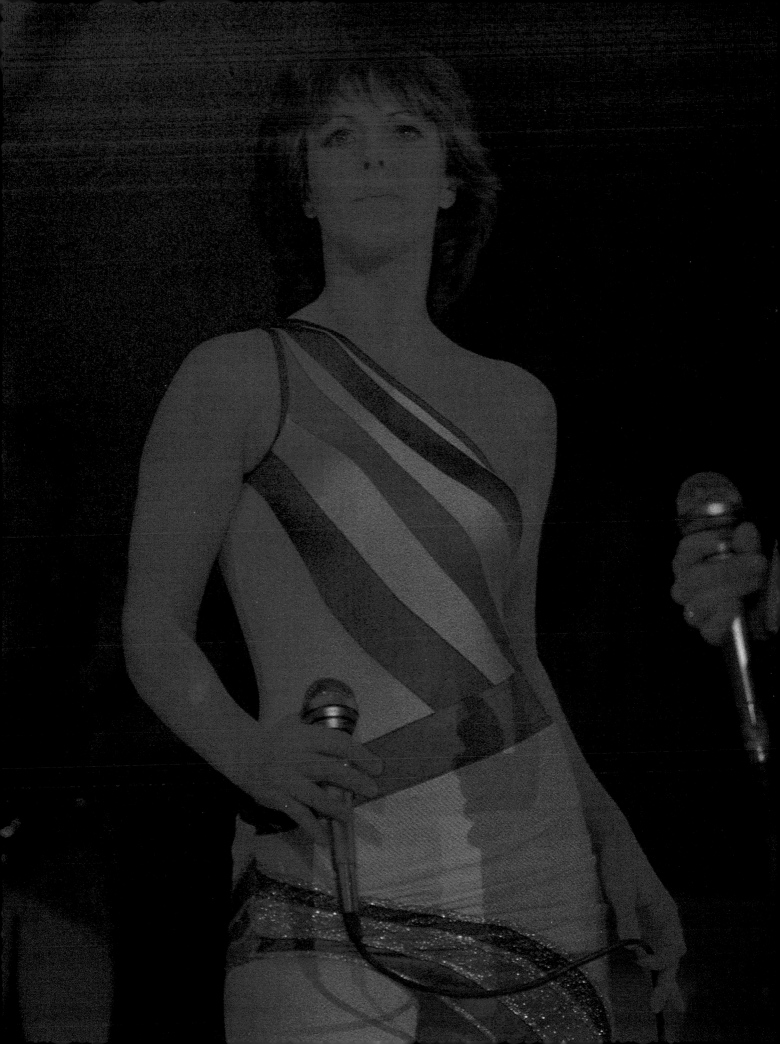

December 7th, 1979
I HAVE A DREAM/TAKE A CHANCE ON ME (Epic EPC 8088)

ABBA's last single of the 1970s was something of a rush release. As the group wrote on the lavish picture sleeve, "November 1979 will always be full of fond memories of our UK tour. Releasing this single gives us the opportunity to thank the thousands of you who made our visit so memorable. In 1979, *The Year Of The Child*, 'I Have A Dream' had a special meaning for us and enabled us to perform the song with choirs of British school-children who joined us on stage each night. Together with our song 'Take A Chance On Me', as performed live at Wembley, we hope this will be an ideal souvenir of our time in Britain."

Evidently it was: within a matter of days, the single had entered the charts at No.21, and within two weeks, had reached No.2 – an almost perfect way to end an incredibly successful decade, during which ABBA had climbed from obscurity to become the biggest record sellers of all time. More than 150 million ABBA records were estimated to have passed over shop counters around the world during the 1970s!

1980

Following the highly successful tour, the quartet returned to normal life, although only briefly – Benny and Björn spent much of January in warmer climes, Barbados to be precise, where they started preparing material for a new album. Meanwhile, Agnetha and Frida were engaged on a somewhat different task, the results of which would be heard later in the year when the 'Gracias Por La Musica' album was released. In the spring, the ABBA touring machine reassembled for a three week tour of Japan, before starting on the serious business of recording an album to follow 'Voulez-Vous'.

July 18th, 1980
GRACIAS POR LA MUSICA (LP) (Epic EPC 86123)
Side One: GRACIAS POR LA MUSICA *[THANK YOU FOR THE MUSIC]*/ REINA DANZANT *[DANCING QUEEN]*/AL ANDAR *[MOVE ON]*/DAME! DAME! DAME! *[GIMME! GIMME! GIMME! (A MAN AFTER MIDNIGHT)]*/ FERNANDO
Side Two: ESTOY SONANDO *[I HAVE A DREAM]*/MAMMA MIA/HASTA MANANA/ CONOCIENDOME, CONOCIENDOTE *[KNOWING ME, KNOWING YOU]*/CHIQUITITA

At the start of the year, while Benny and Björn were writing new songs, Agnetha and Anni-Frid were re-recording some of their best-known vocals in Spanish for this album particularly tailored for the South American market. On their return from the West Indies, Björn and Benny mixed the tracks, which had been engineered by Micke Tretow, and the album was swiftly released in countries in that predominantly Spanish-speaking continent. Spanish lyrics were again written by Buddy & Mary McCluskey, whose translation of the words to 'Chiquitita' had been so successful less than a year before. McCluskey explained how it all started: "I work in Argentina for RCA, the record company for ABBA in that territory. Mary, my wife, and I wrote a Spanish translation of 'Chiquitita', and the girls re-recorded the vocals. It was a hit, and then I started helping them out with their Spanish accents". McCluskey also explained how sometimes translations were less than precise, citing 'Gimme! Gimme! Gimme!', which can be immediately translated to 'Dame! Dame! Dame!', although 'A Man After Midnight', when literally translated, becomes the rather clumsy 'Un Hombre Despues De Medianoche'. Instead, the snappier 'Amor Esta Noch' ('love tonight') was used, and something similar also happened with 'Thank You For The Music'. Somewhat surprisingly, the Spanish album also sold well in Japan, much to the amazement of everyone at Polar in Stockholm, and perhaps it was this unlikely success that led to it being released in Britain – after all, how many non-Spanish speaking ABBA fans could really be expected to want an album sung in Spanish? Eventually, it came out in the UK just one week before the first new ABBA single for over seven months – perhaps the idea was to remind the fickle record buyers that ABBA were still around. There was no need to worry...

July 25th, 1980
THE WINNER TAKES IT ALL/ELAINE (Epic EPC 8835)

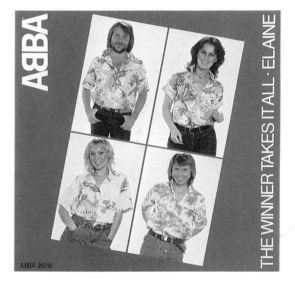

This was not only ABBA's first new single for some time, it also restored them to the top of the British singles chart for the first time in nearly two and a half years, during which time they had released half a dozen Top 5 singles, none of which had reached that crucial Number One spot. This was one of Benny and Björn's more reflective songs, with lyrics which suggested some regret at the end of a relationship, perhaps mirroring the split between Agnetha and Björn. In 1992, during an interview with Alex Duval-Smith in *The Guardian*, Björn confirmed "It was quite true that our lives were reflected in the lyrics – one can't help that – though that doesn't mean a song like 'The Winner Takes It All' is autobiographical; neither Agnetha nor I were winners in our divorce". A familiar name was missing from the long-serving rhythm section, with drummer Ola Brunkert joined by bass player Roger Palm, playing behind Benny on keyboards, guitarist Lasse Wellander and percussionist Ake Sundqvist, although the faithful Rutger Gunnarsson was still involved, this time as string arranger. The B-side of the single, 'Elaine', was yet another of those tracks which was not issued on an album at the time. The single entered the chart a week after release at No.9, and the following week was at Number One, where it remained for a second week before being replaced by David Bowie's remarkable 'Ashes To Ashes', his second chart-topper, which interestingly referred back to his only previous UK Number One, 'Space Oddity', mentioning that the well-known fictional astronaut, Major Tom, was in fact a drug addict! Even so, the ABBA hit remained in the chart for 10 weeks, and also reached the Top 10 of the US pop charts.

November 14th, 1980
SUPER TROUPER/THE PIPER (Epic EPC 9089)

With massive advance sales of the forthcoming new album, the release of a second Number One single was a predictable master stroke. The title of 'Super Trouper' refers to a hugespot light used by ABBA (and many other top pop and rock acts) during stage performances. This track was accompanied by a spectacular video filmed in a circus big top. The original idea behind this novel approach might have been even more innovative, but the Police refused to allow the video to be filmed in Piccadilly Circus in central London. Their reluctance was not only explained by the need to avoid the potential traffic chaos which might result when it became known that ABBA would be visible in the middle of London's West End, but also because there are restrictions on the use of animals in central London. While it would no doubt have made sensational headlines had a circus animal somehow escaped into Leicester Square (the nearest grassy area), it was perfectly understandable that such a risk couldn't be entertained under any circumstances – even for ABBA! The video was eventually filmed in a Stockholm film studio.

The single entered the UK chart the day after release at No.13, jumped to No.2 the following week, when it just failed to unseat Blondie's irresistible 'The Tide Is High', but by the end of November was in the top spot, where it remained for three weeks, until it was overwhelmed by John Lennon's '(Just Like) Starting Over'. The Lennon single had entered the chart one week before 'Super Trouper', and seemed to have peaked just inside the Top 10; it was dropping in the chart until Lennon was killed in New York, whereupon it swiftly rose again, reaching Number One just before Christmas. In a list of the biggest selling singles of 1980, both 'The Winner Takes It All' and 'Super Trouper' were featured among the Top 30 of the year.

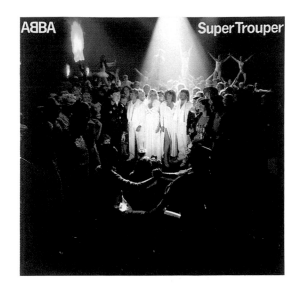

November 21st, 1980
SUPER TROUPER (LP) (Epic EPC 10022)
Side One: SUPER TROUPER/THE WINNER TAKES IT ALL/ON AND ON
AND ON/ANDANTE, ANDANTE/ME AND I
Side Two: HAPPY NEW YEAR/OUR LAST SUMMER/THE PIPER/
LAY ALL YOUR LOVE ON ME/ THE WAY OLD FRIENDS DO

ABBA's name was still very much in the headlines by the time the new album emerged in early November, and advance sales of over one million units were enough to ensure that it entered the UK chart at Number One, where it remained for nine weeks, until it was overtaken by John Lennon's comeback album, 'Double Fantasy', which had entered the chart on the same day as 'Super Trouper'. It is a tribute to the exceptional quality of 'Super Trouper', possibly ABBA's finest original album, that it retained the top position for six weeks after Lennon's assassination, despite the huge public sympathy for the dead Beatle. Among the other musicians (apart from the quartet featured on 'The Winner Takes It All') who played on various tracks on the album were drummer Per Lindvall, Rutger Gunnarsson on bass, guitarist Janne Schaffer, three saxophone players on 'On And On And On', Janne Kling (flute on 'The Piper') and, of course, Björn on acoustic guitar. The final track was a live version, recorded at Wembley the previous autumn, of 'The Way Old Friends Do', a studio-recorded version of which seems never to have been released. Both this song and 'Happy New Year' perhaps seem somewhat sentimental, but their unforgettable melodic brilliance made up for any lyrical shortcomings. This writer's favourite track from the album has always been 'Our Last Summer', a joyful reflection sung from the point of view of a woman who can never forget the summer she spent in Paris with a boyfriend named Harry (a football fan, who went on to work in a bank). A superb chorus with perfect vocal harmonies and a guitar solo of heroic proportions by Lasse Wellander make it a timeless pop/rock classic. Many of the other tracks on the album, especially 'Lay All Your Love On Me' and 'On And On And On', attracted considerable commercial success in other parts of the world when they were released as singles.

December 5th, 1980
SUPER TROUPER (BOX SET) (ABBOX 1)

This limited edition item was briefly released for a matter of only days, although several thousand copies were sold in the period before Christmas, 1980. As well as the chart-topping album, the box also contained a large colour poster of ABBA and a copy of the album-sized biography of the group, *ABBA For The Record* – you are reading a fully updated version of that book.

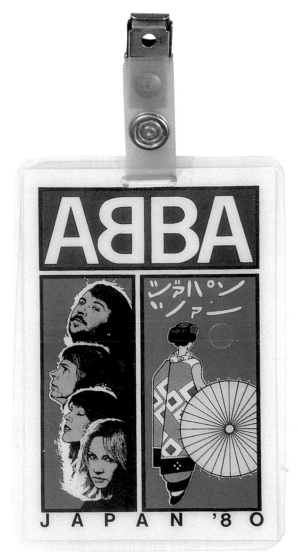

1981

Januar 25th, 1981, Stig Anderson achieved a milestone – his 50th birthday, when the four members of ABBA dressed in the clothes they had worn when they won the Eurovision Song Contest in 1974. A great deal had happened in the intervening seven years, bringing incredible international success, but also personal heartache. To commemorate this momentous event, Benny and Björn wrote and recorded a special song, 'Salute To Stig', which is probably the rarest ABBA record of all, as only 200 copies were pressed as red vinyl 12" singles. Also in January, Björn married Lena Kallersjo, in a ceremony so secret that the first Stig Anderson knew of it was when he was asked by a Swedish newspaper for a comment. Once again, happiness for one part of ABBA was swiftly followed by sadness for another – in February, Anni-Frid and Benny announced that they would be filing for divorce. How could the world-dominating quartet continue after yet another body blow?

In April, 1981, the quartet starred in a TV special made in America and hosted by Dick Cavett, both talking with Cavett and performing several live songs – some of the latter would appear many years later on the 'ABBA Live' album. Björn answered Cavett's criticism that ABBA's lyrics were somewhat mundane compared to the exceptional quality of their music by saying "We used to use the words as something you needed to sing the melody, and they didn't mean very much to us, but I would say that the lyrics on the last two albums have improved – we try to put more feeling into them".

Also in 1981, a solo album by Agnetha, 'Tio Ar Med Agnetha', was released in Sweden. It contained a selection of tracks from her Swedish language albums released in the previous ten years – the album's title can be translated as 'Ten Years With Agnetha'.

July 10th, 1981
LAY ALL YOUR LOVE ON ME/ON AND ON AND ON
(Epic EPC A 13 1456)

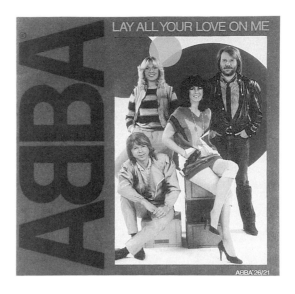

In the absence of any new material – it had, after all, been only a matter of months since the emergence of the 'Super Trouper' album – it was decided to couple these two album tracks as a single, although there was a very good reason for their selection. Both tracks, released separately, had been remixed and in their more disco-oriented style, had topped the US disco (dance or club) chart, and it was felt that to combine them on a single in Britain would attract interest, despite the fact that literally millions of record-buyers already owned them as part of the album. In order to make it an even more attractive purchase, the single was not released in normal 7" format, but only as a 12" 45. By this time, there was a feeling in the pop press (which seemingly disapproves of any act remaining popular for longer than a few months) that ABBA had been too big for too long, and *Melody Maker's* singles reviewer, while managing to make a reference to the heavily publicised forthcoming wedding of the Prince of Wales, wrote: "Over a Euro-disco backdrop, the two perfect couples weave their anthemic magic. A lovely record for Prince Charles to put on the royal turntable before consummating the wedding of all time. Lady Di should love it". It was another example of ABBA's incredible popularity: the single reached the Top 10 of the UK chart, becoming the highest-placed single ever (up to that time) to only be available in 12" format, peaking at No.7, and spending seven weeks in the UK chart.

In September, the group were honoured guests at the annual convention of CBS Records (the Epic label is part of the CBS 'Family') in Bournemouth, and there was news of a brand new album nearing completion. During their short visit, Björn and Benny met Jaap Eggermont, the Dutchman who conceived and produced the hugely successful Starsound, whose 'Stars On 45' was one of the biggest hits of 1981. The 'Stars On 45' concept, which Eggermont used on several internationally successful tracks, was to create a medley of well-known hits performed by Dutch musicians whose aim was to create a sound almost identical to the original recordings, but with a disco beat underpinning the sound to make it irresistible on the dance floor. The first 'Stars On 45' hit medley was largely comprised of hits by The Beatles, but it wasn't long before Starsound were tackling an ABBA medley, which unsurprisingly sold extremely well. Titled 'Stars On 45 Vol.3', it was the third 'Stars On 45' hit single and reached the UK Top 20. The ABBA medley included 'Voulez-Vous', 'S.O.S.', 'Bang-A-Boomerang' (originally on the 1975 album, 'ABBA'), 'Money, Money, Money', 'Knowing Me, Knowing You', 'Fernando', 'The Winner Takes It All' and 'Super Trouper'.

October 23rd, 1981
ABBA (LP) (Epic EPC 32052)

CBS Nice Price Series. An identical reissue of EPC 80835, originally released on June 7th, 1975.

In November, Benny returned briefly to England, more precisely to Doncaster, where he purchased two 3 year old thoroughbred racehorses, Secret Army and Hurtwood Lass. Benny also married his girlfriend, Mona Norklit, during the month. It later transpired that He had been struck by seeing Mona appearing on television, and had made strenuous efforts to meet her. Within a short time, they had fallen in love, and this had been the major reason for Frida and Benny separating. Also during the autumn of 1981, Benny and Björn attended a pop summit meeting with Tim Rice, the lyricist behind such hugely successful musicals as *Joseph And His Amazing Technicolour Dreamcoat, Jesus Christ Superstar* and *Evita,* all of which he wrote with Andrew Lloyd Webber, who supplied the melodies to Rice's words. His meeting with the ABBA masterminds was to discuss the exciting possibility of a collaboration which would come to fruition by 1984...

December 4th, 1981
ONE OF US/SHOULD I LAUGH OR CRY
(Epic EPC A 1740)

This was the first track to be heard from ABBA's ninth (and last) original album, and once again, seems to suggest regret in its lyrics about the end of a relationship. With mandolin parts credited to 'The Three Boys' (who were actually Björn, Lasse Wellander and Rutger Gunnarsson), this is an ABBA classic, and the single's failure to reach Number One may have had much more to do with the timing of the release than with its quality – despite the usual brilliant video clip (which featured Agnetha), with only three weeks until Christmas, the single had insufficient time to gain the momentum needed to overtake both 'Don't You Want Me' by The Human League and Cliff Richard's revival of the Shep & The Limelites classic, 'Daddy's Home'. However, one unique feature of this single was that it was also released in picture disc form, thus becoming the first ever ABBA picture disc single. Not, however, the first ABBA picture disc ever released in Britain – that honour is claimed by a very limited edition of the 'Voulez-Vous' album as a picture disc. Limited? So limited that no-one remembers when it was released, or how many were pressed...

December 11th, 1981
THE VISITORS (LP) (Epic EPC 10032)
THE VISITORS/HEAD OVER HEELS/WHEN ALL IS SAID AND DONE/ SOLDIERS/I LET THE MUSIC SPEAK/ONE OF US/TWO FOR THE PRICE OF ONE/SLIPPING THROUGH MY FINGERS/ LIKE AN ANGEL PASSING THROUGH MY ROOM

With a Top 3 hit single in the bag, this album was inevitably going to be successful, although in comparative terms, a chart residency of 21 weeks including three weeks in pole position was quite a comedown after the 43 chart weeks accumulated by 'Super Trouper', which was at Number One for nine weeks. However, the album also entered the album charts of Holland, Sweden, Belgium and Denmark at Number One, which made it an instant success in commercial terms. Nevertheless, in all honesty, this album, when judged by ABBA's previously impeccable standards, was comparatively disappointing, a feeling reinforced by its short UK chart life. There were fewer singles released from 'The Visitors' than from any original ABBA album since 'Waterloo', and it seemed that perhaps the almost constant pressure (and the requirement for a new album every year, with its attendant globe-trotting promotional schedule) along with the

sad divorces, had taken its toll. The sleeve picture told its own story – Agnetha stands looking at a book (a visitor's book?), while Frida is seated centre stage. Björn stands looking glum, and Benny sits relaxed. None of them is looking at any of the others, and only Benny seems to be looking at the camera. This photograph contains little happiness, and several of the songs seem far more serious than those usually found on an ABBA record, and more like songs by serious rock artists – Björn and Benny had progressed from perfect pop songs and romantic bliss in the late 1970s to the harsh realities of changes in musical fashions and separation from their longterm partners. The album's title track, featuring Frida's lead vocal, was quite a departure for ABBA, telling a story about someone waiting for an inevitable visit from someone who will "take" them and "break" them – the police? But why? Death? Surely not... A most un-ABBA-like song, and almost in the style of another world-famous group whose members had once been married, but were now divorced, Fleetwood Mac. 'When All Is Said And Done' is a song about the end of a romance, with a resigned air which once more accurately reflected the traumas of the quartet's personal relationships. 'Soldiers' is rather obscure lyrically, but sounds magnificent musically, with impressive vocal harmonies – perhaps the lines "they look so strong, you'd think that nothing in the world was wrong" are the key to the song's meaning; rather less meaningful than the chorus which proclaim "soldiers write the songs that soldiers sing..." Björn later indicated that the soldiers referred to in the song were not simply the military rank and file, but more those in decision-making positions. 'I Let The Music Speak' is very ambitious musically, although the song sounds rather like something from a theatrical work, as does 'Head Over Heels' (see below), both leaning towards the typical popular music of continental Europe rather than that of Britain or America. In an interview with *Songwriter* magazine, the ABBA songwriting duo attributed their worldwide success to having been brought up on American and English rock'n'roll as well as German 'schlager' music and Italian schmaltz, and taking the best from each...

Perhaps the most unlikely song on the album is 'Two For The Price Of One', which is sung by Björn. The story of a man who is looking for a girlfriend and dials a telephone number he finds in a 'lonely hearts' advertisement, it contains a fairly unpredictable punchline, and would not seem out of place on an album by the Manchester hitmakers of the 1970s, 10cc. Until the release of 'Lay All Your Love On Me'/'On And On And On', this track, which was one of the first completed for the album, was considered for possible single release – it is certainly different enough... 'Slipping Through My Fingers' is a ballad which was surely conceived specifically for Agnetha, who takes lead vocal. With lyrics about children growing into teenagers, its sentimental approach seems at odds with the many more adventurous songs on the album, while the closing 'Like An Angel Passing Through My Room' is sung by Frida to the accompaniment of a ticking clock (generated by a synthesiser), and most of the track was recorded with only Frida and Benny in the studio. Agreeing with a suggestion that there are major differences between the previous 'Super Trouper' album and 'The Visitors', Frida said: "Since our divorces, we have become more mature, and our style is progressing more quickly than before. 'The Visitors' reflects this evolution, this maturity".

The musicians who played on the album included several familiar names – Ola Brunkert on drums (apart from on 'Soldiers' and the title track of the album, on which Per Lindvall is the drummer), Rutger Gunnarsson on bass, Lasse Wellander on guitar and Ake Sundqvist (percussion), plus Jan Kling playing flute and clarinet on 'I Let The Music Speak'.

At the end of a momentous year, the Christmas album featuring Agnetha and her daughter, Linda, was released in Sweden. Titled 'Nu Tandas Tusen Juleljus', it contained traditional Christmas songs sung in Swedish.

On January 3rd, 1982, Björn and Lena's first child, Emma, was born, and exactly a week later, on January 10th, Benny and Mona were celebrating the birth of Ludwig (doubtless named after Beethoven, the famous classical composer).

Björn and Benny discuss arrangements

February 5th, 1982
HEAD OVER HEELS/THE VISITORS (Epic EPC A 2037)

1982

Agnetha takes the lead vocal on this, the second single released from the new album, with its fairground-styled musical backing courtesy of Benny. Not really a pop song, it seems more of a theatrical item, like several other ABBA songs of this era. The video clip for this single featured Frida wearing a variety of interesting costumes. The B side of the single was the album's title track, and Frida's favourite from the album: "It's a little bit different from all the rest. I think the lyrics on the album are much better than before, more sophisticated". This was the first ABBA single in Britain since 1975 which failed to reach the Top 10 – in fact, it didn't even make the Top 20, peaking at No.25 and only featuring in the chart for a brief seven weeks. It was a result of the fact that 'The Visitors' was the first ABBA album to include so few potential singles – no more tracks from it were released in single form.

The August 1982 issue of International ABBA Magazine reprinted a feature published in *Songwriter* magazine the previous year about ABBA's manager, Stig Anderson. The preamble to the interview noted that ABBA had overtaken The Beatles as the biggest-selling group in pop history, adding that as one of the richest corporations in Sweden, Polar Music might soon be listed on the Swedish stock exchange. Stig explained that when he wrote songs with Benny and Björn, the melody always preceded the lyrics: "When we agree that the melody is there, then I start thinking of lyrics. I believe it's

important to get a catchy international title which people can remember in Hong Kong, Switzerland and Brazil – you must remember that in Brazil, they don't speak English. We look at Sweden as one of the countries of the world – we don't care more about Sweden than any other country. We care about England, Germany, France and Japan because they are much bigger markets". Asked about Polar Music, Stig noted: "We have so many offers from big artists and big record companies in the States to produce records for them, but the problem with ABBA is that Björn and Benny have to be in the group when it's touring, and when we are in the studio, they have to be there singing and producing. If Björn and Benny were free from ABBA, we could do so many other things".

In a companion feature, also in *Songwriter* magazine, Björn and Benny also disclosed their songwriting methods. They wrote either at Benny's house, during the summer at a cottage owned by the group on an island outside Stockholm, or in the attic at the Polar offices. They write regularly, keeping "more or less office hours – we start on Monday morning at 10 or 11 and write until 4 o'clock, and we go on for the whole week". Early inspiration came from songwriters like The Beatles (their favourite songwriters), The Beach Boys (that group's leader, Brian Wilson, was Benny's early favourite), and Jerry

Leiber & Mike Stoller (who wrote songs for Elvis Presley, The Coasters among others), but more recently, they had tried to start from the point where previous songs ended. If Björn starts a lyric and Benny doesn't like it, it isn't used. They write songs which are more personal, and aren't afraid to share with others feelings they have experienced themselves. Björn, who disclosed the fact that he now thinks in English when writing lyrics, also noted that 'Happy New Year' was about "trying to set positive goals for the future. It's as close as we've come to writing something really political".

During the late summer of 1982, Frida's first solo album to be released worldwide, 'Something's Going On', appeared, following a single which was effectively the album's title track, 'I Know There's Something Going On'. The single became a minor hit, peaking just outside the UK Top 40, and was written by Russ Ballard, whose songs had previously provided hits for many artists, including Hot Chocolate ('So You Win Again', a 1977 chart-topper) and Rainbow ('Since You've Been Gone', a big hit in 1979). The B side of the single was another track from the album, 'Threnody' (the title means funeral song and this is not exactly a song, more a poem, written by American satirist Dorothy Parker and set to music). The album, which was produced by Genesis member/solo star Phil Collins, was recorded in Stockholm at Polar Studios. Frida had been impressed by a Phil Collins solo album, 'Face Values', particularly because he also had just suffered the rigours of a divorce – which was largely the inspiration behind his album.

The 'Something's Going On' album also included 'You Know What I Mean', a song written by Collins, 'Tell Me It's Over' by Stephen Bishop, 'I've Got Something' by Tomas Ledin (who sang 'Not Bad At All' as a featured song on the 1979 ABBA tour), 'I See Red', written by Jim Rafferty (brother of Gerry Rafferty, whose 'Baker Street' has now become a standard), 'Baby Don't You Cry' by Rod Argent (on which Collins enlisted assistance from the horn section of the US R&B group, Earth, Wind & Fire, who had also guested on his album), 'Strangers' by Jayne Bradbury & Dave Morris from Birmingham group Jealous Girl, who were signed as songwriters to ABBA's British music publishers, Bocu Music, 'To Turn The Stone' by Giorgio Moroder (which was Frida's favourite track on the album), 'Here We'll Stay' (on which Frida duets with Phil Collins), and 'The Way You Do', written by Bryan Ferry. Apart from Collins playing drums, the other main musicians who appeared on the album were Peter Robinson (keyboards), Mo Foster (bass) and Daryl Stuermer (guitar). The album featured in the UK chart for seven weeks, its highest position being just inside the Top 20.

Benny and Björn finished writing two new songs for ABBA, 'Just Like That' and 'I Am The City', for the next album, which was reported to include 26 tracks – 24 singles, a new track released as a single to coincide with the album, and one completely new track, perhaps one of the two mentioned.

(Bottom Left) Björn with Tim Rice

August 13th, 1982
SUPER TROUPER/THE WINNER TAKES IT ALL/
ONE OF US/LAY ALL YOUR LOVE ON ME
(Epic EPC A 40-2618 cassette single)

The reason for the release of this curious item surely had little to do with ABBA. It was probably released at a time when the UK record industry was making one of its periodic attempts to launch a new format, (in this case, the cassette single). Shortly afterwards, it was probably forgotten.

During the summer, Frida went on a promotional trip taking in the USA, Canada, the UK, Denmark, Germany, Holland, France and Spain to stimulate extra interest in her album, while Agnetha released a single titled 'Never Again', a duet with Tomas Ledin, who had ironically written a song which Frida had included on her album. Frida also released a single in France, a duet with Daniel Balavouine titled 'Belle', which used the tune of ABBA's 'Arrival'.

October 8th, 1982
THE DAY BEFORE YOU CAME/CASSANDRA (Epic A 2487)

Released a month before the double album anthology of ABBA's singles, this was a commercial disappointment, faring even less well than 'Head Over Heels' at the start of the year. A mere six weeks in the chart with a highest position of 32 was hardly cause for huge celebration, but when one learns that the two singles which topped the UK charts during that six week period were 'Do You Really Want To Hurt Me' by Culture Club and 'I Don't Wanna Dance' by Eddy Grant, the ABBA single probably seemed like a dated anachronism. However, the British electropop duo, Blancmange, released their version of 'The Day Before You Came' in the summer of 1984, and it peaked just outside the UK Top 20 – outperforming the ABBA original by ten places.

November 5th, 1982
THE SINGLES – THE FIRST TEN YEARS
(Double LP) (Epic ABBA 10)
Side One: RING RING/WATERLOO/SO LONG/I DO, I DO, I DO, I DO, I DO/
S.O.S./MAMMA MIA/FERNANDO
Side Two: DANCING QUEEN/MONEY, MONEY, MONEY/KNOWING ME,
KNOWING YOU/THE NAME OF THE GAME/TAKE A CHANCE ON ME/
SUMMER NIGHT CITY
Side Three: CHIQUITITA/DOES YOUR MOTHER KNOW/VOULEZ-VOUS/
GIMME! GIMME! GIMME! (A MAN AFTER MIDNIGHT)/I HAVE A DREAM
Side Four: THE WINNER TAKES IT ALL/SUPER TROUPER/ONE OF US/
THE DAY BEFORE YOU CAME/UNDER ATTACK

No 'Lay All Your Love On Me' or 'Head Over Heels'? Neither track was released as a single in every country where the album was released, and thus could not be included on a compilation album designed for worldwide release. The launch party for the album (with several hundred invited guests) was held at the Belfry Club in Belgravia, where ABBA were presented with an award which is surely unique – a huge frame containing gold versions of all 23 singles featured on the album. The album itself was inevitably an immediate success, quickly moving to the top of the UK chart in the second week of its chart run of 22 weeks – only one week longer than 'The Visitors', but the new album, of course, was a double, and thus might be said to have been twice as successful. Another track which had been released as a single but was omitted from this compilation is 'Angeleyes', which was listed as a double A side with 'Voulez-Vous'. However, the inclusion of two brand-new tracks, 'The Day Before You Came' and 'Under Attack', probably more than atoned for the lack of the three obvious missing tracks (and maybe also 'I've Been Waiting For You', the flip of 'So Long', which was also regarded as a double A side). The double album, on which the tracks were arranged chronologically, also illustrated how Björn had largely taken over the writing of ABBA's lyrics – Stig Anderson was involved in helping to write nine of the first 11 songs on the album, the last single to which he contributed being 'The Name Of The Game'.

New Musical Express reviewer Richard Cook wrote: "This isn't the entire history of pop over the last ten years, but its documentation of the group who altered the course of pop more than anyone else – anyone – is flawless", calling the tracks on the album: "a seam of unbroken, highly individual pop music that in lifespan terms is still unmatched by any rival". There is very little more to say about this album, apart from the fact that it sold prodigiously – no big surprise, as it contained virtually every big hit released by ABBA. It couldn't fail – and it didn't.

December 3rd, 1982
UNDER ATTACK/YOU OWE ME ONE (Epic EPC A 2971)

The other newly-recorded track included on the double album was a bigger hit than its predecessor, at least peaking within the UK Top 30, if not the Top 20. This seems to have been the final track for which ABBA made a video, and although it was far from the group's finest commercial moment, it was a perfectly respectable final single from an act which had dominated the world's charts for the previous nine years – the reference to ten years in the album's title could be justified by the continental European success of its opening track, 'Ring Ring'...

December 10th, 1982
THE SINGLES – THE FIRST TEN YEARS (Epic ABBOX 2)

The chart-topping double album released only five weeks before, but this time in a box which also contained a specially written 12 page booklet and a reproduction of a ticket to the 1974 Eurovision Song Contest at Brighton where ABBA first conquered Britain. This limited edition maintained interest in the double album, and doubtless helped to consolidate its chart position.

On January 20th, 1983, Agnetha started recording her first English language solo album at Polar Studios in Stockholm.

1983

February 18th, 1983
SUPER TROUPER/LAY ALL YOUR LOVE ON ME/
THE WINNER TAKES IT ALL/ONE OF US
(Epic EPC A 2618)

Having released a cassette single featuring these four tracks six months earlier, a four track vinyl single now emerged. It is difficult to think of any credible reason for its release at this time, although no doubt it was in response to demand, but insufficient demand, unfortunately, for it to reach the UK chart.

During the spring of 1983, Frida moved her home base from Stockholm to London.

March 11th, 1983
THE VISITORS (CD) (Epic EPC CD10032)

This was almost certainly the first ABBA album released on CD in Britain.

Tomas Ledin (the ABBA live backing vocalist who had duetted with Agnetha on 'Never Again') married Stig's daughter, Marie Anderson, on May 22nd, 1983, and among the guests at the reception were Agnetha, Benny with Mona and Björn with Lena. Anni-Frid was away, but sent a congratulatory telegram.

Mike Chapman with Agnetha

May 27th, 1983
SUPER TROUPER (CD) (Epic EPC CD10022)
GREATEST HITS (CD) (Epic EPC CD10017)

With the introduction of the new digital format, two big selling classics from ABBA's remarkable catalogue of hit albums were also released on CD.

On June 3rd, 1983, Agnetha's first English language solo album, 'Wrap Your Arms Around Me', was released in the UK. It had been recorded earlier in the year at Polar Studios in Stockholm with Micke Tretow engineering, and was produced by Australian-born Mike Chapman. Chapman had been very successful as producer of Blondie, before which he was half of the famed Chinnichap team, who wrote and produced numerous hits during the 1970s with The Sweet, Mud, Suzi Quatro and others. It was originally announced that the album would include Agnetha's famous song featured on the 1979 tour, 'I'm Still Alive', but eventually that idea was abandoned, and instead, she wrote a new song, 'Man', which was also released as the B side of the second of the three hit singles taken from the album, none of which reached the Top 30 of the UK chart. Chris Norman, Alan Silson and Terry Uttley, three quarters of Smokie, another act whom Chapman had produced with great success in his Chinnichap days, supplied backing vocals on much of the album, which included two songs, 'I Wish Tonight Could Last Forever' and 'Can't Shake Loose' (the latter was also the third single), written by Russ Ballard (who had also written 'I Know There's Something Going On' for Frida's album), plus two songs by Tomas Ledin. The first (and biggest) single from the album was 'The Heat Is On'. Also during the year, Agnetha recorded 'P&B', the title song of a Swedish feature film, and it was released as one side of a huge hit single in Sweden, the other side of which was 'It's So Nice To Be Rich'. However, the single was not released in Britain. During what was obviously a very busy year for her, Agnetha also appeared in a Swedish film, 'Raskenstam'.

July 22nd 1983
ARRIVAL (LP) (Epic EPC 32320)

CBS Nice Price Series. An identical reissue of EPC 86018, originally released on November 5th, 1976.

September 16th, 1983
THE SINGLES – THE FIRST TEN YEARS (2 x CD)
(Epic ABBA CD10)

The double CD version of the chart-topping album, which made it clear that the new format had not really been considered when the vinyl version was conceived. The total running time of all 23 tracks was over 92 minutes, very generous for a double vinyl album, but too long for a single CD (with maximum capacity of around 75 minutes) and rather short for a double CD (with capacity of around 2½ hours). Nevertheless, it was a big success, simply because it contained so many classic hits.

On October 1st, 1983, ABBA were accorded a unique compliment when the Swedish Post Office issued a set of five commemorative stamps, each with a picture of notable Swedish musicians. One of these stamps featured ABBA, without any doubt the most internationally successful Swedish popular musicians ever.

Also at the end of a year which had seen little collective ABBA activity, but work on individual projects, a musical, *ABBAcadabra*, was staged at London's Lyric Theatre in Hammersmith. It was based on ABBA's songs and starred Elaine Paige and Scottish singer/songwriter B.A.Robertson – Frida recorded a duet with Robertson of 'Time', a song from the show, and it was released as a single which became a minor UK chart hit around Christmas, 1983. Like Frida's duet with Daniel Balavouine, this song's melody was based on the ABBA instrumental, 'Arrival'. In 1985, an 'ABBAcadabra' album was released in France, featuring three tracks on which Frida participated. The album eventually sold nearly a million copies in France, but was very rarely, if ever, seen in Britain.

November 4th, 1983
THANK YOU FOR THE MUSIC/OUR LAST SUMMER
(CBS A 3894)

After the huge success of the double album, the release of another ABBA compilation for the Christmas record token market was almost obligatory, and this single coupling two classic album tracks was designed to publicise the album via the airwaves. It performed its task very well, even becoming a minor hit single in its own right and peaking at No.33 in a six week stay in the chart. It was glowingly reviewed in *Melody Maker* by Stephen Luscombe and Neil Arthur, better known collectively as Blancmange. Luscombe noted: "Immaculate as per usual" and continued "They're better looking than a Volvo and they sound nicer as well", while Arthur added "Thanks a million, ABBA, for giving it to me! I really like this – they can re-release it as many times as they want as far as I'm concerned". During the summer of the following year, Blancmange scored their eighth UK hit single with a cover version of ABBA's 'The Day Before You Came', surely proof that they really did admire the Swedish quartet's music.

November 4th, 1983
THANK YOU FOR THE MUSIC (LP) (Epic EPC 10043)
Side One: MY LOVE, MY LIFE/I WONDER (DEPARTURE)/HAPPY NEW
YEAR/SLIPPING THROUGH MY FINGERS/FERNANDO/ONE MAN,
ONE WOMAN/EAGLE
Side Two: I HAVE A DREAM/OUR LAST SUMMER/THE DAY BEFORE
YOU CAME/CHIQUITITA /SHOULD I LAUGH OR CRY/THE WAY OLD
FRIENDS DO/THANK YOU FOR THE MUSIC

With four tracks ('Fernando', 'I Have A Dream', 'The Day Before You Came' and
'Chiquitita') also included on 'The Singles – The First Ten Years', this album could be
said to have been a missed opportunity. Why did it omit 'Head Over Heels', 'Lay All Your
Love On Me' and the other tracks released as singles which weren't on the double
album? The four tracks from 'The Album' were easily available, and so were most of the
others on various original albums. Why weren't some of the single B sides that hadn't
been on albums chosen? Ultimately, it made little difference in terms of sales though, the
album featuring in the UK album chart for nearly three months, and reaching the Top 20.

1984

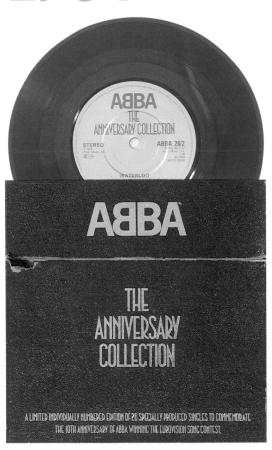

April 2nd, 1984
THE ALBUM (LP) (Epic EPC 32321)

CBS Nice Price Series. An identical reissue of EPC 86052, originally released on January 13th, 1978.

April 9th, 1984
BOXED SET OF 26 SINGLES (ABBA 26/1)

Released to commemorate ABBA's Eurovision Song Contest victory almost exactly ten years before (April 6th, 1974), the boxed set included every ABBA single released in the UK up to this time, 25 of which had reached the chart in the previous ten years – had the title of the double album released 18 months earlier really been so quickly forgotten? Unsurprisingly, as it was fairly expensive, the box of hits failed to reach the UK singles chart, not least because it was produced as a limited edition in blue translucent vinyl and doubtless only designed to appeal to avid collectors.

Frida's second English language solo album, 'Shine', was released by Epic Records on vinyl and cassette in October, 1984, but was not released on CD in Britain until early 1993. Recorded in France and produced by Steve Lillywhite, who had experienced considerable success with acts like Simple Minds, U2, Peter Gabriel and Big Country, the album charted in Britain for a single week, and included songs written by Stuart Adamson (of Big Country), Chris Rea and Kirsty MacColl (who is also Mrs. Steve Lillywhite, but is a noted songwriter with several major hits to her credit). There was even a track written by Benny and Björn, 'Slowly'...

October 30th, 1984
LAY ALL YOUR LOVE ON ME (Epic EPC A 131456)

A reissue of the single which had topped the US dance chart and reached the UK Top 10 back in 1981. This time, it failed to chart.

(Opposite page) Frida meets French fans
(Top) ABBA on US TV show

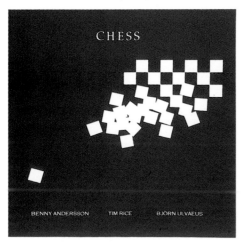

November, 1984
CHESS – Original Sound Track Recording (Double Album)
RCA PL/PK/PD 70500(2)

This magnificent collaboration between Benny and Björn, who wrote the music, and Tim Rice (with assistance from Björn), who wrote the lyrics, was very successful, remaining in the UK album chart for four months and peaking in the Top 10. It included two very substantial single hits, 'One Night In Bangkok' by Murray Head, which peaked just outside the Top 10 at the end of 1984 (but topped the charts in much of the rest of Europe and reached the Top 3 in the US), and 'I Know Him So Well', a duet between Elaine Paige and Barbara Dickson, which held the Number One position in Britain for four weeks at the start of 1985. This song's success made Benny and Björn only the tenth producers to achieve ten Number One singles! A single was also released between these two hits, Elaine Paige's 'Nobody's Side', but this did not feature in the UK chart.

The musical was indeed about chess, the board game, and concerned a fictional love story about a Russian chess champion who fell in love with a woman from a Western country. In 1982, a world chess championship was contested in a hotel in Iceland between an American, Bobby Fischer, and a Russian, Boris Spassky, and as this was at a time when the Cold War between the superpowers of America and Russia was still in full swing, the political implications of even a game of chess were significant. Clearly not an obvious subject for pop, *Chess* nevertheless proved to anyone who still doubted that the ABBA duo's work could be taken seriously that they rank with the all-time greats as song craftsmen. As well as Elaine Paige (who for many years was very close to Tim Rice), Barbara Dickson and Murray Head, other performers on the 'Chess' album included Denis Quilley (a well-known British actor), Tommy Korberg (a Swedish performer whose work was highly acclaimed by the critics) and Björn Skifs, while many familiar names were found among the backing musicians: Lasse Wellander (guitar), Per Lindvall (drums), Rutger Gunnarsson (bass), Anders Eljas and Benny (of course) on keyboards, and backing vocalists brother and sister Anders & Karin Glenmark, who in 1985 released an excellent album titled 'Gemini', which was produced by Benny and Björn. The dynamic duo also contributed several songs they had written to the 'Gemini' album, one of which was 'Just Like That', a song which ABBA had recorded back in 1982 for possible inclusion on 'The Singles – The First Ten Years', but which was eventually not used on that package. The 'Chess' album was produced by Benny, Tim Rice and Björn, and recorded at Polar Studios with Micke Tretow as engineer. Tim Rice told Terry Wogan on BBC Television that he made 41 trips to Stockholm during the recording of the album! The album was also notable for the fact that it featured the London Symphony Orchestra working alongside the Swedish pop and rock musicians – a most potent combination indeed!

November 19th, 1984
ARRIVAL (C) (Epic CD86018)
THE ALBUM (CD) (Epic CD86052)
VOULEZ-VOUS (CD) (Epic CD86086)

'Arrival', 'ABBA – The Album' and 'Voulez Vous' were three more digital versions of these past hit albums.

In February, 1985, Björn and his wife Lena and their family moved to a large house with 16 acres of land in England, near Henley in Oxfordshire.

April 15th, 1985
GREATEST HITS (Epic EPC 32571)

CBS Nice Price Series. An identical reissue of EPC 69218, originally released on March 26th, 1976.

Agnetha's second solo album, 'Eyes Of A Woman', was released by Epic Records on vinyl and cassette in April, 1985, with a CD version following in June, 1985. The album was produced by Eric Stewart of the highly successful English group, 10cc. The first and most successful single from the album, 'I Won't Let You Go', was co-written by Agnetha and Eric Stewart, but it did not reach the UK chart. Among the other songwriters whose work can be heard on the album were Jeff Lynne (ELO, Traveling Wilburys among others), Justin Hayward (Moody Blues) and John Wetton & Geoff Downes (of Asia). In a promotional interview sent out with the album to reviewers, Agnetha said of the ABBA

1985

years: "Together, we have been through good and bad things. I don't want that period undone, but I don't want to start it all over again", adding "Maybe I could imagine doing another album, but nothing more".

In view of the fact that ABBA had dominated the world's charts for much of the previous ten years, it was somewhat surprising that they did not play at Live Aid. Perhaps they were invited, but declined, for the usual reasons of not having enough time to prepare a live show – every other live appearance by the group had been carefully prepared and rehearsed, and this may have represented an insuperable problem.

OPUS 10

During this year, Benny, Björn and Frida, who were all in London for the launch of a new album by Elaine Paige, announced that there would be a new ABBA album, which would be recorded in 1986. The working title for this seems to have been 'Opus 10' (as it would have been the tenth original ABBA album), and it was scheduled to included an instrumental title track and 'Just Like That', the song which was originally recorded as a possible new track for 'The Singles – The First Ten Years', back in 1982. Frida also declared that she was abandoning her solo career, and would return to ABBA – had anyone asked Agnetha if she would take part?

1986

I n January, 1986, the four members of ABBA worked together for the first time in several years, causing great excitement amongst all fans. They recorded a filmed tribute to 'the fifth member of ABBA', Stig Andersson, which formed part of a *This Is Your Life* TV show about their erstwhile manager. They sang a Swedish song written by Stig in the 1940s titled 'Tived – Shambo'.

1986 also brought another duet from Agnetha. This time she recorded with Ola Hakanson, a member of the well-known Swedish group, Secret Service. The song, 'The Way You Are', was written as a theme for the Olympic Games and was also featured in a Swedish movie.

The *Chess* musical opened at London's Prince Edward Theatre on May 14th, 1986, and was extremely successful, running for several years. Hailed by the critics, the show proved equally popular with the British public. By the time of the première, Frida, who attended the opening along with numerous other personalities, had moved her main residence to Zurich in Switzerland.

August 4th, 1986
VOULEZ-VOUS (LP) (Epic EPC 32322)

CBS Nice Price Series. An identical reissue of EPC 86086, originally released on May 4th, 1979.

Despite the suggestion during the previous year that a brand new ABBA album would be recorded, nothing emerged. Perhaps the continued absence of Agnetha made such a project an impossibility...

March 1987
THE HITS (LP) (Pickwick SHM 866)
WATERLOO/S.O.S./DANCING QUEEN/KNOWING ME, KNOWING YOU/
LAY ALL YOUR LOVE ON ME/ SUPER TROUPER/TAKE A CHANCE ON ME/
I DO, I DO, I DO, I DO, I DO/HONEY HONEY/ HASTA MANANA/
THE VISITORS/MAMMA MIA

1987

A budget priced album released on vinyl and cassette undoubtedly including many hits, although 'Mamma Mia' was the only one of the last five tracks which was a substantial hit – each of the four tracks preceding it was less notable than the eight genuine hits which were the album's major selling point.

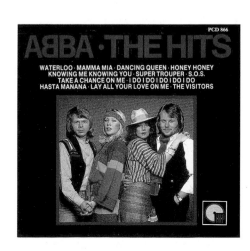

May 18th, 1987
GREATEST HITS VOL. 2 (LP) (Epic EPC 450915-1)

CBS Nice Price Series. An identical reissue of EPC 10017, originally released on May 4th, 1979.

(Left) *Look-In* magazine strip cartoon of the ABBA story
(Below) Björn, Agnetha, Anni-Frid and Benny reading the ABBA magazine – some covers featured right

ABBA Magazine No.15 40p

Holiday Special

See Abba Live-Win Tickets For Abba's Autumn Shows

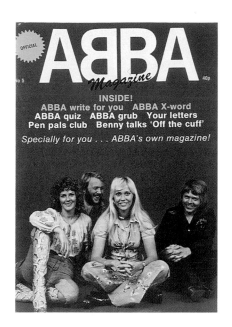

OFFICIAL **ABBA** Magazine No 5 40p

INSIDE!
ABBA write for you   ABBA X-word
ABBA quiz   ABBA grub   Your letters
Pen pals club   Benny talks 'Off the cuff'

Specially for you . . . ABBA's own magazine!

ABBA magazine # 33 50p

The Lennon Legacy
Super Trouper — Your Reviews
Fan Focus,   "The Mystery Tour"
Plus News, Puzzles, Competition
Results and more.

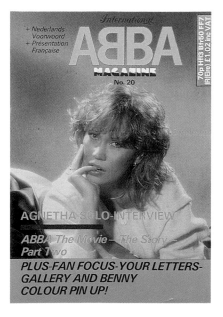

International **ABBA** MAGAZINE No. 20

+ Nederlands Voorwoord
+ Présentation Française

70p Hfl3 Bfr50 FF7 IR(8)p £1.02 inc VAT

AGNETHA SOLO-INTERVIEW

ABBA The Movie — The Story —
Part Two

PLUS-FAN FOCUS-YOUR LETTERS-
GALLERY AND BENNY
COLOUR PIN UP!

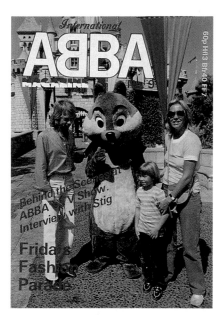

International **ABBA** MAGAZINE 60p Hfl3 Bfr40 FF7

Behind the Scenes at
ABBA TV Show.
Interview with Stig

Friday Fashion Parade

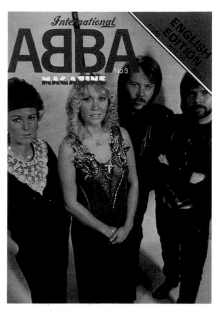

International **ABBA** MAGAZINE No3 ENGLISH EDITION

ENGLISH EDITION No 4 £0.60 Hfl2.50 Bfr40 **ABBA** MAGAZINE

ABBA magazine 35 50p

ABBA as you have never seen them,
when Polar Have a Party.
The South American Scene,
Interview and Discography.

ABBA magazine # 36 50p

The Meeting of Minds —
ABBA's Assistant Comes to Town

Plus Puzzles, Discography, News
and Poster Competition

During 1987, Agnetha recorded and released an album with Christian, her son (whose father was Björn). Titled 'Komm Folj Med I Var Karussell', it was an album of children's songs, and was a major success in Sweden, following her previous duet album with her daughter, Linda, in 1980. Agnetha also released her third English language solo album, 'I Stand Alone', during the year. Although it was hardly promoted outside Scandinavia, the album, which was produced by Peter Cetera of the highly successful American rock group Chicago, actually outsold Madonna's then current album in Sweden, and reached the UK album chart for a single week in March, 1988.

Frida also enjoyed a solo hit in Sweden with 'Sa Lange Vi Har Varann', on which she was backed by the Swedish group, Ratata, and it was also recorded in English titled 'As Long As I Have You'. She was featured as part of the choir who sang on the title track of a solo album by Benny which mixed folk songs and classical music, 'Klinga Mina Klocker'. The song in question was written by Björn.

From the early days (bottom left) to the 80s, various Agnetha Fältskog picture sleeves

September 1987
THE HITS (CD) (Pickwick PCD 866, later re-numbered PWKS 593)
WATERLOO/S.O.S./DANCING QUEEN/KNOWING ME, KNOWING YOU/
LAY ALL YOUR LOVE ON ME/ SUPER TROUPER/TAKE A CHANCE ON ME/
I DO, I DO, I DO, I DO, I DO/HONEY HONEY/ HASTA MANANA/
THE VISITORS/MAMMA MIA

A budget-priced CD version of the album released six months earlier. This was almost certainly the first ABBA album released on CD at budget price.

December, 1987
ABBA – THE COLLECTION (2 x CD) (Castle CCSCD 176)
WATERLOO/THE NAME OF THE GAME/THE WINNER TAKES IT ALL/
DANCING QUEEN/SUPER TROUPER/FERNANDO/GIMME! GIMME! GIMME!
(A MAN AFTER MIDNIGHT)/S.O.S./I HAVE A DREAM/DOES YOUR MOTHER
KNOW/VOULEZ-VOUS/ANGELEYES/RING RING/THE DAY BEFORE YOU
CAME/HEAD OVER HEELS/THANK YOU FOR THE MUSIC/I DO, I DO, I DO,
I DO, I DO/UNDER ATTACK/ARRIVAL/HONEY HONEY/THE VISITORS/
ROCK ME/EAGLE/DANCE (WHILE THE MUSIC STILL GOES ON)

An interesting collection, starting with six Number Ones and ending with six non-hits. Its failure to chart came as no real surprise – at this point, ABBA seemed to have been forgotten by British record buyers. This album was probably the first by ABBA to be simultaneously released on vinyl and cassette – subsequent entries in this book will refer to CD catalogue numbers in the case of simultaneous releases on CD, vinyl and cassette.

February, 1988
THE HITS II (CD) (Pickwick PWKS 500)
THE NAME OF THE GAME/ARRIVAL/RING RING/EAGLE/SUMMER NIGHT
CITY/HAPPY NEW YEAR/ANGELEYES/MONEY, MONEY, MONEY/
ANDANTE ANDANTE/VOULEZ-VOUS/KISSES OF FIRE/THE DAY BEFORE
YOU CAME/WHEN I KISSED THE TEACHER/FERNANDO

Another somewhat inaccurately titled budget-priced CD – five of the 14 tracks here were
big hits, many of the others weren't hits at all – but like its predecessor from the previous
year, extremely successful.

July 4th, 1988
THE ALBUM/VOULEZ-VOUS (CD)
(Epic CDABA 241)

A twofer CD – two albums on CD for the price of one (as the catalogue number
suggests). Doubtless a marketing concept – two classic hit albums packaged together at
a bargain price – which included many other artists whose catalogue was controlled by
the CBS group at the time.

September, 1988
THE COLLECTION VOLUME 2 (2 x CD) (Castle CCSCD 198)
DANCING QUEEN/TAKE A CHANCE ON ME/I HAVE A DREAM/DOES YOUR MOTHER KNOW/ CHIQUITITA/RING RING (BARA DU SLOG EN SIGNAL)/ ANOTHER TOWN, ANOTHER TRAIN/ DISILLUSION/PEOPLE NEED LOVE/ I SAW IT IN THE MIRROR/NINA, PRETTY BALLERINA/ THANK YOU FOR THE MUSIC/TWO FOR THE PRICE OF ONE/FERNANDO/GIMME! GIMME! GIMME! (A MAN AFTER MIDNIGHT)/SUPER TROUPER/WATERLOO/ LOVE ISN'T EASY (BUT IT SURE IS HARD ENOUGH)/ME AND BOBBY AND BOBBY'S BROTHER/HE IS YOUR BROTHER/ SHE'S MY KIND OF GIRL/ I AM JUST A GIRL/ROCK N ROLL BAND

The first British release of two previously unheard ABBA albums found them packaged as a double. The complete 'Ring Ring' album is on sides two and four, while the incomplete 'Live' album – the full album has three more songs – is on sides one and three. The tracks were licensed from Polygram, the multi-national corporation which includes such record companies as Polydor, Phonogram, London, Island and A&M, among others, who were in the process of purchasing Polar Music from Stig Anderson. Castle Communications asked to license material for a second Collection double album, but Polygram decided that these two albums, which had never previously been available in Britain other than as imports, would be an appropriate choice. While it is true that the idea had commercial merit, it seems clear to ABBA fans that the two albums in question may be incompatible. 'Ring Ring' was the very first ABBA album, recorded in 1973 and including few tracks which had been heard by fans of ABBA's singles, whereas the live tracks had been recorded either in 1977 during an Australian tour, in 1979 at Wembley in London, or on the televised *Dick Cavett Show* in the US during 1981, and featured many of the best known ABBA hits, as well as the ultra-sophisticated 'Two For The Price Of One'. Apart from the potential incompatibility point (not to mention the cost of a double album), few seemed aware of the existence of this release, and it did not reach the UK chart.

September, 1988
THE HITS VOLUME III (CD) (Pickwick PWKS 507)
THE WINNER TAKES IT ALL/THE KING HAS LOST HIS CROWN/DANCE (WHILE THE MUSIC STILL GOES ON)/GIMME! GIMME! GIMME! (A MAN AFTER MIDNIGHT)/HEAD OVER HEELS/ROCK ME/I HAVE A DREAM/ CHIQUITITA/THE PIPER/ON AND ON AND ON/ONE OF US/OUR LAST SUMMER/DOES YOUR MOTHER KNOW/THANK YOU FOR THE MUSIC

Probably a better-known selection than the tracks on 'The Hits Volume 2', this was yet another budget-priced CD compilation, which was unsurprisingly successful. However, it should be remembered that each volume of 'The Hits' not only included several big hits, but also a number of tracks which must have been quite obscure to the impulse buyers at whom the albums were aimed.

Around this time, Benny produced an album by the Swedish folk group, Orsa Spelman, also playing on several tracks on the album, two of which appeared on a compilation album titled 'Fiolen Min'.

October, 1988
ABSOLUTE ABBA (2 x CD) (Telstar TCD 2329)
FERNANDO/THE NAME OF THE GAME/CHIQUITITA/THANK YOU FOR THE MUSIC/ANGEL EYES/WATERLOO/KNOWING ME, KNOWING YOU/ONE OF US/DOES YOUR MOTHER KNOW/ SUMMER NIGHT CITY/LAY ALL YOUR LOVE ON ME/THE WINNER TAKES IT ALL/SUPER TROUPER/MONEY, MONEY, MONEY/VOULEZ-VOUS/RING RING/HEAD OVER HEELS/TAKE A CHANCE ON ME/DANCING QUEEN/GIMME! GIMME! GIMME! (A MAN AFTER MIDNIGHT)/ MAMMA MIA/I DO, I DO, I DO, I DO, I DO/S.O.S./ I HAVE A DREAM

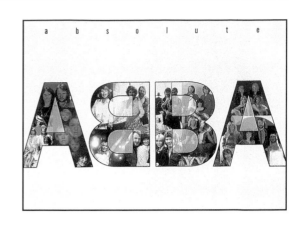

The first sign that British record buyers were still interested in ABBA came when this strong compilation, with 24 genuine hits, was promoted via a TV advertising campaign and spent seven weeks in the UK album chart. Although the highest position it reached was only No.70, the length of time spent in the chart still showed ABBA's appeal had not waned. This was ABBA's first chart album for five years, and their last for another four, when 'Gold' was to restore them not only to the album chart, but also to the Number One position. By the time 'Gold' was released however, Telstar's contract to license the tracks had long expired, and the album had been deleted.

There were rumours that an EP by ABBA containing four new songs, 'Its Been Swell', 'Something On My Mind', 'It's Alright Darling' and 'I Just Wasn't Thinking', would be released shortly before Christmas 1988, but as nothing emerged, it appears that the rumours were sadly inaccurate.

ABBA's original songwriting trio collect yet another award

1989

March 6th, 1989
THE ALBUM (CD) (Epic EPC CD32321)
VOULEZ-VOUS (CD) (Epic EPC CD32322)

The two albums which had been previously released in single packages, were reissued separately at mid-price (a fate which eventually befalls every album – even ABBA albums).

Benny released a second solo album, titled 'November 1989', which was even more classically-oriented than 'Klinga Mina Klocker', and included a song sung by Tommy Korberg, 'The Conductor' – Korberg had been featured on the 'Chess' album several years before.

December, 1989
THE LOVE SONGS (CD) (Pickwick PWKS 564)
Side One: UNDER ATTACK/SLIPPING THROUGH MY FINGERS/SHOULD I LAUGH OR CRY/GONNA SING YOU MY LOVE SONG/LOVERS (LIVE A LITTLE LONGER)/LOVELIGHT/I'VE BEEN WAITING FOR YOU
Side Two: MY LOVE, MY LIFE/ONE MAN, ONE WOMAN/TROPICAL LOVELAND/ANOTHER TOWN, ANOTHER TRAIN/WHEN ALL IS SAID AND DONE/IF IT WASN'T FOR THE NIGHTS/SO LONG

Another budget-priced compilation, although this time with no major hits. However, this 14 track collection was doubtless snapped up by ABBA fans, even though every track had previously appeared on CD – at this price, 'The Love Songs' certainly seemed like a great bargain.

The first day of 1990 was the formal date on which Polygram acquired the ABBA catalogue and Polar Music from Stig Anderson, for an undisclosed (but obviously huge) price. Major changes such as this, often prompt a close look from all sides at the pluses and minuses of the new situation. There was no doubt that the the members of ABBA and the Polar organization with Stig in the chair, was a close-knit club and this relationship between longtime friends and partners was bound to change with the new corporate ownership.

The group, and no doubt, Stig too, probably felt that they were now on the outside looking in; the catalogue now belonged to Polygram and the group members therefore had no further influence or control on the future direction for ABBA.

On a more positive note though, the start of the new decade was also the point at which ABBA's recorded heritage was the property of a single, multi-national record company worldwide for the first time ever. This presented a golden opportunity to develop the back catalogue, which was packed with so many songs that had been incredibly popular in the late 70s and early 80s, and which were still instantly recognisable around the world. Certain licensing arrangements were still in operation several years later however, with a variety of record companies who had released material and whose licenses had yet to run their full course. Polygram were therefore unable to use the catalogue with absolute freedom until well into the decade, although as recent events have shown, their re-release of the hits via 'ABBA GOLD' has proved to be a huge success around the globe and on a scale that could not perhaps have been foreseen.

Benny and Björn wrote a theme song for a horse riding championship, 'Upp Till Kamp',

An interesting and probably freezing photo session, Norway, 1977

which was recorded and again featured vocals by Tommy Korberg. Benny also released an album during the year, but this was not an album on which he played – it featured the sounds of Swedish birds singing, and was beautifully packaged.

An unusual accolade for ABBA came in November, 1990, when a music student at Cambridge University, Philip Lodge, won an award of £150 for his analysis of the group's songs in an essay. Philip, whose tutors describe him as a brilliant musician, is also, hardly surprisingly, an enthusiastic fan of ABBA. He told a British newspaper: "I have great respect for their skills." Lodge cited the parallelism in ABBA's music, which he likened to that of Mozart.

On December 15th, 1990, Agnetha married Tomas Sonnenfeld, a Swedish surgeon, in a church near her mansion on the island of Ekero, near Stockholm.

I n 1991, Benny wrote two new songs, 'Lassie' and 'Alska Mej', for The Ainbusk Singers, a Swedish group composed of four girls. However, Björn and Benny, one of the worlds most successful song writing teams was still very much in action, writing a song for Kalle Moreaus called 'Beatrice'.

1991

It was suggested that a 4CD boxed set of ABBA recordings was to be released in 1992, although eventually this idea was postponed.

Björn returned to live in Sweden at the end of the year, while incorrect gossip suggested that Agnetha was pregnant – but that the father was not her husband, Tomas, it was supposedly an American actor with the unlikely name of Rory Emerald. Agnetha also mentioned that she was not intending to continue with her singing career.

1992

On January 28th, 1992, Frida joined the Swedish group Roxette onstage in Zurich in Switzerland and they performed 'Money, Money, Money' together.

April 9th, 1992
RING RING (CD) (Polydor 843 642-2)

RING RING/ANOTHER TOWN, ANOTHER TRAIN/DISILLUSION/PEOPLE NEED LOVE/I SAW IT IN THE MIRROR/NINA, PRETTY BALLERINA/ LOVE ISN'T EASY (BUT IT SURE IS HARD ENOUGH)/ME AND BOBBY AND BOBBY'S BROTHER/HE IS YOUR BROTHER/SHE'S MY KIND OF GIRL/I AM JUST A GIRL/ROCK'N'ROLL BAND

Never released as an individual album in Britain before this time, nearly 20 years after it was recorded, this album was presumably aimed at ABBA collectors rather than the mainstream market. Which is not to suggest that it is bad, but rather that it represents the very first attempts by the group to make international rather than local hits, and as such is to some extent less mature than later, more accomplished work. As a document of the recording birth of a legend, it is extremely valuable – and it's quite easy to enjoy as well!

WATERLOO (CD) (Polydor 843 643-2)
ABBA (CD) (Polydor 831 596-2)

MAMMA MIA/HEY, HEY, HELEN/TROPICAL LOVELAND/S.O.S./MAN IN THE MIDDLE/BANG-A-BOOMERANG/I DO, I DO, I DO, I DO, I DO/ ROCK ME/INTERMEZZO NO.1/I'VE BEEN WAITING FOR YOU/SO LONG/ WATERLOO/HASTA MANANA/HONEY, HONEY/RING RING/ NINA, PRETTY BALLERINA

The last five tracks on this CD were not on the original 'ABBA' album, and it appears that they were added to the album some time before the release date above to increase the playing time of the original 11 track album. All five extra tracks had appeared on the original 'Greatest Hits' album, which had not been reissued by Polydor at the time of writing.

Dear Subscriber,

It is with regret that I have to announce that this issue No.24 of the International Abba Magazine will be the last for the time being. We thank you for your past support and interest in Abba.

By way of re-imbursement for your outstanding subscription we enclose with this last issue some extra goodies.

Inside a unique folder bearing a special drawing of Abba by reader Pat Twist there is a Limited Edition colour print or number of prints, depending on how many issues your subscription has outstanding.

Each print is an exclusive shot finished on high quality glossy paper. After this use the internegs will be destroyed. Subscribers only are receiving this limited edition pack, it is not and will not be offered to the public.

I hope you have enjoyed reading the Abba Magazine over the past six years (not bad going for any publication, let alone one of this type). It is with sadness that we close but with anticipation that we may, one day, be able to publish again.

Yours sincerely,

Charlie

Charlie Bates.

P.S. Back issues of the magazine will still be available from the usual address. See page 28.

ARRIVAL (CD) (Polydor 821 319-2)
THE ALBUM (CD) (Polydor 821 217-2)
VOULEZ-VOUS (CD) (Polydor 821 320-2)
SUPER TROUPER (CD) (Polydor 800 023-2)
THE VISITORS (CD) (Polydor 800 011-2)
ABBA LIVE (CD) (Polydor 829 951-2)
DANCING QUEEN/TAKE A CHANCE ON ME/I HAVE A DREAM/DOES YOUR MOTHER KNOW/CHIQUITITA/THANK YOU FOR THE MUSIC/TWO FOR THE PRICE OF ONE/FERNANDO/GIMME! GIMME! GIMME! (A MAN AFTER MIDNIGHT)/SUPER TROUPER/WATERLOO/MONEY, MONEY, MONEY/ NAME OF THE GAME/EAGLE/ON AND ON AND ON

This live album included tracks from the Wembley shows of 1979 ('Dancing Queen' to 'Thank You For The Music', 'Waterloo' and 'Name Of The Game'/'Eagle'). 'Two For The Price Of One', 'Gimme! Gimme! Gimme!', 'Super Trouper' and 'On And On And On' came from the 1981 *Dick Cavett TV Show*, and 'Fernando' and 'Money, Money, Money' from the Australian leg of the 1977 tour. This excellent live album (which proved beyond all doubt that ABBA were equally adept on the road and in the studio) was the only genuinely new album in this programme of reissues. The album was also released on vinyl, although the final three tracks were omitted, this shortfall only occurring for marketing purposes – at the time, as the record industry began its campaign to boost CD at the expense of vinyl (virtually completed at the time of writing – vinyl is almost extinct), 'bonus' tracks were offered on many CDs (often also on cassettes). Several of these CD releases may have appeared slightly earlier than the listed release date, but this was when Polydor officially released the bulk of the ABBA original albums.

Benny and Björn wrote a number of songs, including 'Heaven And Hell' and 'Leave It To Love', for Josefin Nilsson, a member of The Ainbusk Singers. Josefin's album was produced by Benny alone, using many of the musicians who were once associated with ABBA, including Lasse Wellander, Rutger Gunnarsson and others. This project is intended to result in a complete album of songs by Benny and Björn, probably to be released in 1993.

During June, 1992, British electropop duo Erasure topped the British singles chart with an EP titled 'ABBA-esque', their tribute to ABBA, who were among their favourite groups during their formative years. The EP included 'Lay All Your Love On Me', 'S.O.S.', 'Take A Chance On Me' and 'Voulez-Vous', performed in Erasure's trademark Hi-NRG style. The EP was also a big hit in many other countries. Erasure (keyboard mastermind Vince Clarke and outrageous vocalist Andy Bell) were longtime ABBA fans, having grown up during the period when ABBA was the world's biggest group. Clarke & Bell had originally planned to record an entire album of ABBA songs, but due to an intensive touring schedule, were only able to record four tracks. What's the betting they do a whole album one day?

AGNETHA FÄLTSKOG   I STAND ALONE

On June 11th, 1992, the world famous Irish group, U2, performed a concert at The Globe Theatre in Stockholm, where Benny and Björn joined them onstage for a unique version of 'Dancing Queen', which the group had been including in many concerts on their tour.

A Swedish group called One More Time achieved chart success in Holland with a song titled 'Highland'. The group includes Benny's son, Peter Gronvall, and the track was produced by Frida's son, Hans Fredriksson.

Sad news arrived with the death on August 16th of Johan Karlberg, one of Björn's colleagues in The Hootenanny Singers. Johan was 49 years old.

August 24th, 1992
DANCING QUEEN/LAY ALL YOUR LOVE ON ME/THE DAY BEFORE YOU CAME/EAGLE (CD single)
(Polydor 863573-2 or PZCD 231)

Released as a trailer to the forthcoming 'ABBA Gold' album, this four track single restored ABBA to the UK singles chart after an absence of over eight years. Almost certainly intended primarily to create interest in the album, it nevertheless also reached the UK Top 20, peaking at No.16 This modest chart position hardly gave the world notice of the immense success which would shortly follow. While the first two tracks were included on the album, the others, which were also digitally remastered by Micke Tretow, were not on 'ABBA Gold', which made this item very collectable in its own right.

On August 26th, 1992, in Denmark, Frida married Prince Ruzzo Reuss von Plauen, a German architect with whom she had been living for some time at homes in Switzerland (in the town of Fribourg), Sweden and Majorca. A few days before this happy event, on August 14th, Frida had organised a concert in Sweden, the Water Festival, in which she and other Swedish artists performed to raise funds for ecological and environmental causes. In recent years, after reading a book about the destruction of woodland in Sweden, Frida has become a familiar spokesperson for these causes and has devoted much of her time to them, especially to Det Naturliga Steget ('The Natural Step'), a foundation whose aim is to preserve the environment and prevent its deterioration via conservation. She was one of several artists (including Tomas Ledin) in the choir for the recording of 'Anglamark', a charity single to raise awareness of environmental issues. Its B side was 'Saltwater', a song written by Julian Lennon and sung by Frida.

Alongside his other work, Benny has been collaborating with Björn on a musical based on Wilhelm Moberg's classic historical novel, 'Utvandrarna', which was written about early Swedish settlers in North America. This work has been in progess for some time, and it is hoped that it will be complete by the end of 1994.

September 21st, 1992
ABBA GOLD – GREATEST HITS (CD)
(Polydor 517 007-2)

DANCING QUEEN/KNOWING ME, KNOWING YOU/TAKE A CHANCE ON ME/MAMMA MIA/LAY ALL YOUR LOVE ON ME/SUPER TROUPER/I HAVE A DREAM/THE WINNER TAKES IT ALL/MONEY, MONEY, MONEY/S.O.S./ CHIQUITITA/FERNANDO/VOULEZ-VOUS/GIMME! GIMME! GIMME! (A MAN AFTER MIDNIGHT)/DOES YOUR MOTHER KNOW/ONE OF US/THE NAME OF THE GAME/ THANK YOU FOR THE MUSIC/WATERLOO

Re-mastered by Micke Tretow, this hit-filled album restored ABBA to the top of the album charts in many countries throughout the world including Australia, Austria, Denmark, Germany, Ireland, Israel, Italy, Mexico, Portugal, Singapore, Spain, Sweden, Switzerland and the UK in the first two months of its release. Total sales registered by the first week of 1993 totalled an incredible four million units across all formats. By this time it had also amassed nineteen platinum awards and one gold – many more will certainly follow...

Germany was the first country where sales of the album passed the million mark and Britain was close behind with 900,000, while it had accumulated over 300,000 sales in Italy, over 200,000 in Australia, Denmark and Sweden and more than 100,000 in Belgium, Mexico, Holland, Norway, Singapore, Spain and Switzerland. Who could deny that this was a truly international hit album? But what made it so successful?

Firstly, this was the first single (as opposed to double) album by ABBA to feature all nine UK Number One singles, in addition to which it also included six more UK Top 3 hits among its 19 tracks lasting close to the maximum time which can be encompassed on a single CD. That's 15 Top 3 hits, the outstanding four including three more UK Top 10 hits and 'Thank You For The Music', which may be the most universally loved (and most lyrically appropriate) song ever written by Benny and Björn. With Micke Tretow's sparkling digital mastering, many of the tracks sounded better than ever before, especially as the original versions had first been heard on vinyl – inevitably with records as popular as those by ABBA, much-played vinyl copies eventually displayed signs of wear, and this compilation restored (and even arguably improved) the familiar original sound. This album also became the first ABBA collection ever released on DCC (digital compact cassette), a new format being introduced by Polygram.

There was no chance of this album failing to top the UK chart, and it entered the chart at Number One a week after release. Although it quickly relinquished the pole position, this was no great surprise – in the 1990s, Christmas has become more than ever before the time of year when record companies release blockbuster (hopefully) albums by the biggest stars on their artist rosters, and half a dozen artists, including Madonna, Prince, Peter Gabriel, REM and others, all had albums released between October and Christmas. Virtually all the others were brand new original albums, not compilations with no tracks less than ten years old! The ABBA magic had woken from its decade-long slumber.

The group themselves would be the first to admit that both Erasure and Björn Again had greatly assisted in reminding the world of ABBA. Formed in 1989, Björn Again, the Australian quartet who rose to fame through providing something which seems unlikely

to ever happen again, that is, live ABBA concerts, were sued by ABBA because they used ABBA's highly distinctive logo with the backwards 'B'. However, Björn (of ABBA) was later quoted in the *Daily Mirror* as saying: "I think they are great, and the best of luck to them. They deserve to be very successful". Each of the four main members of Björn Again based themselves closely on a member of ABBA: Gavin Edwards is Björn Volvoeus, Peter Smith is Benny Anderwear, Annette Jones is Agnetha Falstart and Tracy Adams is Frida Longstokin; further demonstrating their sense of humour, their debut single was titled 'Erasure-ish' – remember the title of Erasure's chart-topping ABBA tribute, 'ABBA-esque'?

October 26th, 1992
VOULEZ-VOUS/SUMMERNIGHT CITY/GIMME! GIMME! GIMME! (A MAN AFTER MIDNIGHT)/I DO, I DO, I DO, I DO, I DO (CD single) (Polydor PZCD 239)

A follow up single to 'Dancing Queen' was a brave attempt at a time when the 'ABBA Gold' album was selling so prodigiously, and this one was a very minor chart success. However, once again it was of interest to ABBA collectors as it contained two tracks which were not on the album.

November, 1992
ABBA – THE TRIBUTE (Polar 517 465-2)
HASTA MANANA (Army Of Lovers)/KNOWING ME KNOWING YOU (Sanne Salomonsen)/DOES YOUR MOTHER KNOW (Pelle Almgren & Wow Liksom)/THE WINNER TAKES IT ALL (Freda')/DANCING QUEEN (Rob'n'Raz DLC)/EAGLE (Papa Dee)/THE NAME OF THE GAME (Irma)/RING RING (Sator)/S.O.S. (Stonecake)/DUM DUM DIDDLE (Beagle)/ON AND ON AND ON (Mats Ronander)/KING KONG SONG (Electric Boys)

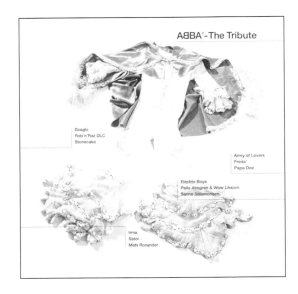

At the end of 1992, as it became clear that ABBA were once again among the most popular acts in the world, a number of well-known Swedish pop and rock stars produced an album titled 'ABBA – The Tribute', which was released in Sweden by Polar Music. While the majority of the names who contributed are probably unknown outside Sweden, three acts, Army Of Lovers, (who enjoyed considerable success around the world in 1991 with such singles as 'Crucified' and 'Obsession'), Sanne Salomonsen (whose 'Where Blue Begins' album was released in the UK by Virgin's Point Blank label) and guitarist Mats Ronander (who was part of ABBA's backing band on their final world tour) are more familiar names.

December 14th, 1992
THANK YOU FOR THE MUSIC/HAPPY NEW YEAR/ THE WAY OLD FRIENDS DO
(CD single) (Polydor PZCD 250)

The fate which awaits this single is not known at the time of writing, but the omens are excellent – could a more appropriate choice of tracks for the end of such a fantastic year be imagined? The group's 'theme', along with a pair of perfect New Year's Eve songs – a great way to start 1993!

Early 1993 saw international discussions taking place about the tracks which should be included on a potential follow-up album to 'ABBA Gold', with project manager Chris Griffin and his assistant Jackie Stansfield at Polygram receiving lists of preferences from all over the world. More delights are expected for ABBA fans – watch this space!

1993

Following the magnificent success of 'ABBA Gold', Polygram, which had also inherited the four solo albums by Annifrid and Agnetha originally released during the first half of the 1980s, reissued all four on CD. Once again, this was the first time that these albums, 'Something's Going On' by Frida from 1982, Agnetha's 'Wrap Your Arms Around Me' from 1983, Frida's 'Shine' (1984) and 'Eyes Of A Woman', Agnetha's 1985 release, had benefitted from a truly international release, and was probably their first appearance in CD format in some territories.

Meanwhile, Polygram's ABBA project manager, Chris Griffin, and his assistant, Jackie Stansfield, were canvassing the various local Polygram companies to discover whether there were special preferences for tracks to be included in the obligatory follow up album to 'ABBA Gold'.

Lively discussion ensued, both on content and title, and an early suggestion for the title, 'ABBA By Request', was considered for several weeks until it was finally decided that the 'Greatest Hits Volume II' album (as it certainly was) should follow the example of its predecessor, which by April 1993, had sold 4.5 million units worldwide (and had still not been released in the USA, potentially a major market). The decision was to stay with a successful formula, and the new album was therefore titled 'More ABBA Gold'.

May 24th, 1993
MORE ABBA GOLD (Polydor 519 353-2)
SUMMERNIGHT CITY/ANGELEYES/THE DAY BEFORE YOU CAME/ EAGLE/I DO, I DO, I DO, I DO, I DO/SO LONG/HONEY HONEY/THE VISITORS/OUR LAST SUMMER/ON AND ON AND ON/RING RING/I WONDER(DEPARTURE)/LOVELIGHT/HEAD OVER HEELS/WHEN I KISSED THE TEACHER/I AM THE CITY/CASSANDRA/UNDER ATTACK/WHEN ALL IS SAID AND DONE/THE WAY OLD FRIENDS DO.

While most dedicated ABBA fans would have been able to predict at least 50% of the 20 tracks selected for this companion volume it was not a second best by any means. Indeed it includes a lot of hits, plus many tracks that would surely have been hits, had they been released as singles.

The one major surprise was the inclusion of a previously unreleased track, 'I Am The City'. This song was written and recorded by ABBA in 1982 and was apparently considered for 'The Singles – The First Ten Years', but eventually not included on that double album. Maybe it would have been on 'Opus 10', the album which ABBA never completed (and perhaps didn't even begin)... nevertheless, the chance to hear a recording by ABBA which had never previously appeared immediately made 'More ABBA Gold' a very desirable purchase, especially as it followed an album which had achieved platinum status in an unbelievable 20 countries and had topped the album charts of a dozen territories.

The album release was accompanied by a special 4 track promotional CD that was exclusively produced for radio stations and clubs. The tracks included were 'Eagle', 'I Am The City', 'I Do, I Do, I Do, I Do, I Do' and 'Ring Ring' and this limited release was widely distributed in a highly successful campaign to gain maximum airplay for 'More ABBA Gold'.

As the sales of the album began to rapidly rise, another promotional single was released in June combining 'Summernight City' with 'I Do, I Do, I Do, I Do, I Do', although neither release was made commercially available.

Sad news was to come with the separation of Agnetha and her husband Tomas Sonnenfeld. Meanwhile Frida appeared on stage in Stockholm with the cast of *ABBA – The True Story*, leaving her seat in the audience to join in with the ABBA anthem 'Thank You For The Music' to the delight of everyone in the theatre.

More delights are expected for ABBA fans all over the world in the coming months and years – watch this space! The ABBA bandwagon continues to roll onwards.......

MORE
ABBA
GOLD

MORE ABBA HITS

DISCOGRAPHY

ABBA

SINGLES

People Need Love/Merry-Go-Round (En Karusell)	1972
He Is Your Brother/Santa Rosa	1972
Love Isn't Easy/I Am Just A Girl	1973
Ring Ring (Bara Du Slog En Signal)/Åh Vilka Tider	1973
Ring Ring (English)/Merry-Go-Round	1973
Waterloo/Honey Honey (both sung in Swedish)	1974
Waterloo(English)/Watch Out	1974
Honey Honey/King Kong Song	1974
So Long/I've Been Waiting For You	1974
I Do, I Do, I Do, I Do, I Do/Rock Me	1975
S.O.S./Man In The Middle	1975
Mamma Mia/Intermezzo No.1	1975
Fernando/Hey, Hey, Helen	1976
Dancing Queen/That's Me	1976
Money, Money, Money/Crazy World	1976
Knowing Me, Knowing You/Happy Hawaii	1977
The Name Of The Game/I Wonder (Departure)	1977
Take A Chance On Me/I'm A Marionette	1977
Eagle/Thank You For The Music	1977
Summernight City/Medley	1978
Chiquitita/Lovelight	1979
Voulez-Vous/Does Your Mother Know – 12"	1979
Does Your Mother Know/Kisses Of Fire	1979
Voulez-Vous/Angeleyes	1979
Gimme! Gimme! Gimme! (A Man After Midnight)/ The King Has Lost His Crown	1979
I Have A Dream/Take A Chance On Me (Live)	1979
The Winner Takes It All/Elaine	1980
Super Trouper/The Piper	1980
Lay All Your Love On Me/On And On And On – 12"	1981
One Of Us/Should I Laugh Or Cry	1981
Head Over Heels/The Visitors	1982
The Day Before You Came/Cassandra	1982
Under Attack/You Owe Me One	1982
Dancing Queen/Lay All Your Love On Me	1992
Voulez-Vous/Summernight City	1992
Thank You For The Music/Happy New Year	1992

ALBUMS

Ring Ring	1973
Waterloo	1974
Abba	1975
Greatest Hits	1975
Arrival	1976
The Album	1977
Voulez-Vous	1979
Greatest Hits Vol.2	1979
Gracias Por La Musica	1980
Super Trouper	1980
The Visitors	1981
The Singles – The First Ten Years	1982
Live	1986
Gold	1992
More ABBA Gold	1993

BENNY & BJÖRN

SINGLES

She's My Kind Of Girl/Inga Theme	1970
Lycka/Hej Gamla Man!	1970
Det Kan Ingen Doktor Hjälpa/På Bröllop	1971
Tänk Om Jorden Vore Ung/Träskofolket	1971
En Karusell/Att Finnas Till	1972

ALBUMS

Lycka	1970
Chess (with Tim Rice)	1982
Chess Original Broadway Cast Recording	1988

BJÖRN

SINGLES

Raring/Vill Du Ha En Vän	1968
Fröken Fredriksson/Vår Egen Sång	1968
Saknar Du Något Min Kära/Gömt Är Inte Glömt	1969
Partaj-Aj-Aj-Aj/Kvinnan I Mitt Liv	1969

Björn by Björn

BENNY ANDERSSON

SINGLE
Klinga Mina Klocker/Långsammazurkan   1987

ALBUMS
Klinga Mina Klockor   1987
November '89   1989

Nov. 80

Benny by Benny

THE HEP STARS

SINGLES
A Tribute To Buddy Holly/Bird Dog   1964
If You Need Me/Summertime Blues   1964
Donna/Farmer John   1965
Cadillac/Mashed Potatoes   1965
Bald Headed Woman/Lonesome Town   1965
No Response/Rented Tuxedo   1965
So Mystifying/Young And Beautiful   1965
Should I/I'll Never Quite Get Over You   1965
Sunny Girl/Hawaii   1966
Wedding/When My Blue Moon Turns To Gold Again   1966
I Natt Jag Drömde/Jag Vet   1966

Consolation/Don't   1966
Malaika/It's So Nice To Be Back   1967
Christmas On My Mind/Jingle Bells   1967
Mot Okänt Land/Någonting Har Hänt   1967
She Will Love You/Like You Used To Do   1967
It's Been A Long Long Time/Musty Dusty   1968
Det Finns En Stad/Sagan Om Lilla Sofi   1968
Let It Be Me/Groovy Summertime   1968
I Sagans Land/Tända På Varann   1968
Holiday For Clowns/A Flower In My Garden   1968
Speleman/Precis Som Alla Andra   1969
Speedy Gonzales/Är Det Inte Kärlek, Säg   1969

ALBUMS
We And Our Cadillac   1965
Hep Stars On Stage   1965
The Hep Stars   1966
Jul Med Hep Stars   1967
Songs We Sang   1968
It's Been A Long Long Time   1968
Hep Stars På Svenska   1969
How It All Started   1970
Hep Stars, 1964-69!   1983
Bästa (CD only)   1990

THE HOOTENANNY SINGERS

SINGLES
Jag Väntar Vid Min Milla/Ann-Margret   1964
Darlin'/Bonnie Ship The Diamond   1964
Den Gyllene Fregatt/Där Skall Jag Bo   1965
Britta/Den Sköna Helen   1965
Solola/Björkens Visa   1965
Den Sköna Helen/Björkens Visa   1965
No Time/Time To Move Along   1966
Marianne/Vid En Biväg Till En Byväg Bor
   Den Blonda Beatrice   1966
Baby, Those Are The Rules/Through Darkness Light   1966
En Sång En Gång För Länge Sen/Det Är Skänt Att
   Vara Hemma Igen   1967
Blomman/En Man Och En Kvinna   1967
En Gång Är Igen Gång/Du Eller Ingen   1967
Mrs O'Grady/The Fugitive   1967
Början Till Slutet/Adjö, Farväl   1967
Så Länge Du Älskar Är Du Ung/Vilken Lycka Att
   Hålla Dej I Hand   1968
Mårten Gås/Du Ska Bara Tro På Hälften   1968
Måltidssång/Till Fader Berg Rörande Fiolen   1968
Elenore/Fåfängans Marknad   1968
Den Som Lever Får Se/Så Länge Jag Lever   1969
Om Jag Kunde Skriva En Visa/Casanova   1969
Vinden Sjunger Samma Sång/Hem Till De Mina   1969
Ring Ring, Här Är Svensktoppsjuryn/Lev Som Du Lär   1970
I Fjol Så Gick Jag Med Herrarna I Hagen/
   Älvsborgsvisan   1970
Rose Marie/Elin Och Herremannen   1970
En Visa Vill Jag Sjunga Som Handlar Om Min Lilla

Vän/Spelmansvisa

Aldrig Mer/Lilla Vackra Anna	1971
Hjärtats Saga/Jungman Jansson	1971
Tess Lördan/Rosen Och Fjärilen	1971
Tiden/Ida & Frida & Anne-Marie	1972
Där Björkana Susa/Calle Schewens Vals	1972
Om Aftonen/Till Min Syster	1973
Brittisk Ballad/Ingrid Dardels Polska	1974
Sjösala Vals/Vals I Valparaiso	1975
Linnea/Fritiof Anderssons Paradmarsch	1975

EP'S

Jag Väntar Vid Min Mila/Ann-Margret/Ingen Enda Höst/Ave Maria No Morro	1964
En Mor/Körsbär Utan Kärnor/Gabrielle/I Lunden Gröna	1964
Lincolnvisan/Hem Igen/Godnattsaga/This Is Your Land	1964
Britta/Solola/Eh Håttespeleman/Telegrafisten Anton Hanssons Vals	1965
Björkens Visa/En Festlig Dag/Vildandens Klagan/ Finns Det Liv Så Finns Det Hopp	1965
Vid Roines Strand/Marianne/En Man Och En Kvinna/Vid En Biväg Till En Byväg Bor Den Blonda Beatrice	1966
Blomman/En Sång En Gång För Längesen/Det Är Skönt Att Vara Hemma Igen/Tänk Dej De' Att Du Och Jag Var Me'	1967
Mårten Gås/Början Till Slutet/Marie Christina/ Adjö Farväl	1967

ALBUMS

Hootenanny Singers	1964
Hootenanny Singers (2nd Album)	1964
Hootenanny Singers Sjunger Evert Taube	1965
International	1965
Many Faces/Många Ansikten	1966
Civila	1967
Bästa	1967
5 År	1968
Bellman På Vårt Sätt	1968
De Bäste Med Hootenanny Singers & Björn Ulvaeus	1969
På Tre Man Hand	1969
Skillingtryck	1970
Våra Vackraste Visor	1971
Våra Vackraste Visor Vol. 2	1972
Dan Andersson På Vårt Sätt	1973
Evert Taube På Vårt Sätt	1974

AGNETHA

SINGLES

Följ Med Mig/Jag Var Så Kär	1967
Slutet Gott, Allting Gott/Utan Dej Mitt Liv Går Vidare	1968
En Sommar Med Dej/Försonade	1968
Den Jag Väntat På/Allting Har Förändrat Sig	1968

Sjung Denna Sång/Någonting Händer Med Mej (Duet with Jörgen Edman)	1969
Snövit Och De Sju Dvärgarna/Min Farbor Jonathan	1969
Fram För Svenska Sommaren/En Gång Fanns Bara Vi Två	1969
Tag Min Hand Låt Oss Bli Vänner/Hjärtat Kronprins	1969
Zigenarvän/Som En Vind Kom Du Till Mej	1969
Skål Kära Vän/Det Handlar Om Kärlek	1969

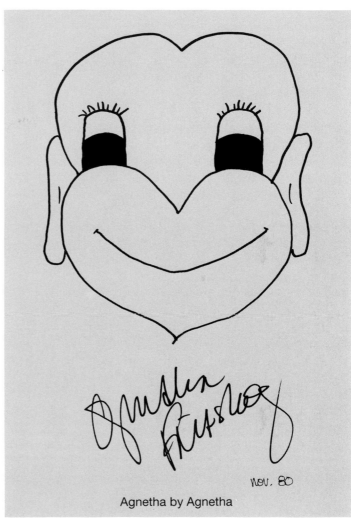

Agnetha by Agnetha

Om Tårar Vore Guld/Litet Solskensbarn	1970
Som Ett Eko/Ta Det Bara Med Ro	1970
En Sång Och En Sanga/Jag Skall Göra Allt	1970
Kungens Vaktparad/Jag Vill Att Du Skall Bli Lycklig	1971
Många Gånger Än/Han Lämnar Mig För Att Komma Till Dig	1971
Nya Ord/Dröm Är Dröm Och Saga Saga	1971
Vart Ska Min Kärlek Föra/Nu Skall Du Bli Stilla	1972
Tio Mil Kvar Till Korpilombolo/Så Glad Som Dina Ögon	1972
Vi Har Hunnit Fram Till Refrängen/En Sång Om Sorg Och Glädje	1973
Golliwog/Here For Your Love	1974
Dom Har Glömt/Gulleplutt	1975
S.O.S./Visa I Åttonde Manaden	1975
När Du Tar Mig I Din Famn/Jag Var Så Kär	1979

Never Again/Just For The Fun (with Tomas Ledin)	1982
The Heat Is On/Man	1983
Wrap Your Arms Around Me/Take Good Care Of Your Children	1983
Can't Shake Loose/To Love	1983
It's So Nice To Be Rich/P & B	1983
I Won't Let You Go/You're There	1985
One Way Love/Turn The World Around	1985
The Way You Are/Fly Like The Eagle (Duet with Ola Håkansson)	1986
Karusellvisan/Liten & Trött (with son Christian)	1987
På Söndag/Min Namn Äv Blom (with son Christian)	1987
The Last Time/Are You Gonna Throw It All Away	1988
Let It Shine/Maybe It Was Magic	1988

GERMAN SINGLES

Robinson Crusoe/Sonny Boy	1968
Senor Gonzales/Mein Schönster Tag	1968
Concerto D'Amore/Wie Der Wind	1969
Wer Schreibt Heut' Noch Liebesbriefe?/Das Fest Der Pompadour	1969
Fragezeichen Mag Ich Nicht/Wie Der Nächste Autobus	1969
Ein Kleiner Mann In Einer Flasche/Ich Suchte Liebe Bei Dir	1970
Geh' Mitt Gott/Tausend Wunder	1972
Komm Doch Zu Mir/Ich Denk' An Dich	1972

ALBUMS

Agnetha Fältskog	1968
Agnetha Fältskog Vol. 2	1969
Som Jag Är	1970
När En Vacker Blir En Sång	1971
Bästa	1973
Agnetha	1974
Elva Kvinnor I Ett Hus	1975
Tio År Med Agnetha	1979
Nu Tändas Tusen Juleljus (with daughter Linda)	1980
Wrap Your Arms Around Me	1983
Eyes Of A Woman	1985
Sjung Denna Sång	1986
Kom Föjl Med I Vår Karusell (with son Christian)	1987
I Stand Alone	1987

FRIDA

SINGLES

En Ledig Dag/Peter Kom Tillbaka	1967
Din/Du Är Så Underbart Rar	1967
Simsalabim/Vi Mots Igen	1968
Mycket Kär/När Du Blir Min	1968
Härlig Är Vår Jord/Räkna De Lyckliga Stunderna Blott	1969
Så Sund Du Måsta Gå/Försök Och Sov På Saken	1969
Peter Pan/Du Betonar Kärlek Lite Fel	1969
Där Du Går Lämnar Kärleken Spår/Du Var Främling	

Här Igår	1970
En Liten Sång Om Kärlek/Tre Kvart Från Nu	1971
En Kväll En Sommarrn/Vi Vet Allt Men Nästan Inget (Duet with Lars Berghagen)	1971
Min Egen Stad/En Gång Är Ingen Gång	1971
Kom Och Sjung En Sång/Vi Är Alla Bara I Början	1972
Vad Gör Jag Med Min Kärlek/Allting Ska Bli Bra	1972
Man Vill Ju Leva Lite Dessemellan/Ska Man	

Frida by Frida

25 nov 1980

Skratta Eller Gråta	1972
Fernando/Ett Liv I Solen	1975
I Know There's Something Going On/Threnody	1982
To Turn The Stone/I've Got Something	1983
Here We'll Stay/Strangers	1983
Belle/C'est Fini (Duet with Daniel Balavoine, France only)	1983
Time/I Am The Seeker (Duet with B.A. Robertson, UK only)	1983
Shine/That's Tough	1984
Come To Me/Slowly	1984
Så Länge Vi Har Varann/Du Finns Hos Mig (with Ratata)	1987
Om Du Var Här/As Long As I Have You (with Ratata)	1987
Änglamark/Saltwater (Artister För Miljö)	1992

ALBUMS

Frida	1971
Min Egen Stad	1972
Frida Ensam	1976
Something's Going On	1982
Shine	1984
På Egen Hand (CD only)	1991

INDEX

ABOUT THE AUTHOR

John Tobler was born in 1943 and educated at Bedford Modern School. After various clerical jobs, he became a computer programmer with National Westminster Bank. In 1967 he began to write for *ZigZag* magazine, which had been started by Pete Frame, with whom Tobler had worked during the early 1960s. During the period between 1967 and 1974 Tobler wrote for various music publications, including *Melody Maker, Disc, Sounds, ZigZag, Record Buyer, Let It Rock* and others. In April 1974, he joined CBS Records as Press Officer, where he originally came into contact with ABBA. At the end of 1975 a freelance career began which has continued until today, taking in writing for *New Musical Express, Record Mirror, Let It Rock, New Music News, Music Week* and many other similar publications both in Britain and Europe.

Tobler worked with the team of BBC Radio One's *Rock On* programme during 1977. Several scripts he wrote were used as the basis for successful radio series, including the prestigious *25 Years of Rock*, a production collaboration between the BBC and *Billboard* magazine. During the mid 1980s he was question setter for the rock mastermind specials, *Rock Brain Of The Universe,* and has worked as a freelance researcher, interviewer and scriptwriter for Radio One series such as *Insight, Rock On Saturday, The Motown Story, The Record Producers* and *The Guitar Greats*. Television and video work includes scriptwriting and researching CCTV's 'Story Of' series, which included *The Story Of ABBA, The Story Of The Bee Gees, The Story Of The Kinks, The Story Of Rod Stewart* and *The Story Of Fleetwood Mac*, which were shown on Channel 4. He was also researcher and associate producer of the 20 volume video series *Rock'n'Roll – The Greatest Years* as well as *Roy Orbison And The Candymen* and *Rod Stewart And The Faces*. Tobler has also contributed to the Video Biography Series, which includes videos on ABBA, The Kinks and The Bee Gees.

Tobler was consultant and commissioning editor to The New Musical Express 'Who's Who In Rock'n'Roll', consultant and contributor to the Orbis partwork 'History Of Rock' and is currently writing 'This Day In Rock' for Carlton. He has also compiled albums and written sleeve notes for record companies such as Polygram, EMI, WEA and CBS, including the sleeve notes for the four million selling 'ABBA GOLD' in 1992. He was responsible for the chart-topping, double platinum 'The Sound Of Bread' compilation in the 1970s and is also Director of the Road Goes On Forever record label.

Among the books which Tobler has written or co-written are '25 Years Of Rock', '30 Years Of Rock', 'The Record Producers', 'The Guitar Greats', 'The Rock Lists Album', '25 Years Of Cliff Richard', 'Elvis – The Legend And The Myth', 'The Beatles', 'The Buddy Holly Story', 'The Doors', 'The Doors In Their Own Words', 'The Clash', 'Punk Rock', 'The Beach Boys', 'Abba For The Record', several pop annuals and volumes of pop quizzes. He was consultant editor to the extremely successful 'NME Rock'N'Roll Years' and is currently writing for *Folk Roots, Country Music People, Billboard, Music and Media* and *Vox*.